POSTSCRIPT SCREENING:
ADOBE ACCURATE SCREENS

Peter Fink

POSTSCRIPT SCREENING: ADOBE ACCURATE SCREENS

Adobe Press
Mountain View
California

Library of Congress Catalog No.: 92-073746

ISBN: 0-672-48544-3

First Printing: September 1992   2 3 4 5 6 7 8 9 10

Adobe Press books are published and distributed by Hayden, a division of Prentice Hall Computer Publishing. For sales, and corporate sales accounts, call 1-800-428-5331.
For additional information, address Hayden, 11711 N. College Avenue, Carmel, IN 46032.

This book is dedicated to Jeanne and Charlie Fink,
without whose help it could not have been written.

Acknowledgments

I've been explaining things for 20 years. So far this book takes the cake. For depth of subject, breadth of audience, and concepts worked out from scratch, no other project comes close. I stopped dreaming about dots months ago—a protective mental reaction set in to save my life.

That which does not kill us makes us strong. Several people became strong as this book gradually emerged over the past year and a half. The following acknowledges other survivors by mentioning them and their contribution in print.

First the Adobe visionaries: Steve Schiller created the Adobe Accurate Screens™ halftoning software. Russell Brown saw the need to explain screening to a wide audience and brought me to Adobe to begin—thank you, Russell! Jim King focused the technology issues and championed the project through its difficult initial stages. Dan Hahn appeared at a key moment and saw the logical outcome as this book on screening—when none of us knew what the book would be or how it would be published. He made it happen.

Meanwhile, Mills Davis and Brigitte Reyes of Davis Inc. put up with my empty office in Washington D.C. and helped Ben Gilbert keep *Desktop To Press*™ going in my lengthening absence. When *Desktop To Press* moved across the country—and then back—Peggy Kaufman not only held the publication together; she made it grow.

Back at Adobe, Rob Babcock and John Kunze provided critical resources. Lars Borg, Mark Donohoe, Grant Ruiz, and Geoff Sherwood, experts all, led me deep into the PostScript Interpreter. Ron Gravatt made the imagesetting equipment produce on time. Bob Greene helped focus the book from the viewpoint of users and developers.

Finally, Patrick Ames of Adobe Press, Mike Britton, Debbie Hanna, and Marj Hopper of Prentice Hall, and editor extraordinaire Judy Helfand. Designers Margery Cantor and Nancy Winters said how the book should be and Michael de Leon actually made it that way. Thank you all.

PETER FINK
ALEXANDRIA, VIRGINIA
AUGUST 1992

Foreword

Preparing and printing a quality color picture with the equipment and tools of graphic arts prepress and print production is a delicate process. The production of a good picture versus a picture that must be redone can hinge on a poor choice for one scanning parameter; the skill of an operator with an image retouching application; the calibration of a scanner, a monitor, an imagesetter, or a press; the choice of spot function for an image full of midtones; the sensitivity of the laser diode in an imagesetter to the temperature in the room; the density characteristics of a particular batch of film; a small adjustment to the blanket of a press; or a slightly bad proportion of ink and water. There is always some blend of technique and art to finesse. None of the many problems that can arise and do are apparent at the end of the print production cycle in a quality color picture.

Few see a quality color picture for what it is. I was explaining to my wife, Renee, that what she sees as a multiplicity of colors in a color picture is really a field of tiny globs of only four colors of ink, meticulously arranged, representing four separate versions of the picture, merged with inking on a printing press to make one color picture that looks as she might expect a color picture to look. She didn't quite believe it, so I handed her a loupe. Her view through the loupe, at the tiny globs, changed her perception of what a color picture is. A tool in her hands opened a new vista.

The technique of screening is evolving. It's more accessible to those not traditionally considered experts, due to the widening availability of standard tools like Adobe Accurate Screens™ technology. Remember a few years ago when it seemed there were as many proprietary prepress front-ends and output devices as there were font foundries and font formats? And how the PostScript™ language with its Type-1 font technology stilled the font cacophony by harmonizing the use of fonts? Screening is going down a similar path. It's becoming more accessible, easier to do, more automatic—democratized.

The ongoing merging of color reproduction and desktop publishing calls for graphic arts savvy in the desktop domain and, PostScript language savvy in the color reproduction domain. *PostScript Screening: Adobe Accurate Screens* fills the need for a book that addresses PostScript screening in a graphic arts prepress and print production context. Author Peter Fink, consultant to the graphic arts prepress and print production communities and author of *Desktop To Press*™, discusses key theoretical and practical aspects of PostScript screening, always with an eye to achieving the best-quality imagesetter and press output. He also addresses, from his own experience, what is required to make effective use of Adobe Accurate Screens technology, the screening technology that is a standard part of the PostScript language.

While less technical readers are welcome and may learn much from *PostScript Screening*, it is first directed to engineers and advanced users who make PostScript screening work for everyone else. Beginners will gain perspective on screening and a broad acquaintance with topics that must be mastered before returning to the book more knowingly. Those with more expert background, will be equipped to develop screen sets for use in preparing high-quality color output.

DAN HAHN
MANAGER, IMAGESETTER ENGINEERING
ADOBE SYSTEMS INCORPORATED
AUGUST 1992

Contents

Chapter Three

PART TWO: THEORY

Chapter Four

Chapter Five

Chapter Six

Chapter Ten

Chapter Eleven

APPENDICES

Introduction

In our culture, visual images have tremendous impact. This impact grows from art and logically extends to business, where getting the pictures right is what matters. Currently, one of the most challenging technical areas in high-quality commercial PostScript language print production is halftoning, also known as screening.

Compelling, well-presented images reward not only the companies that publish them, but also the numerous professionals who have a hand in their creation. You may be one of these professionals, for example, a graphic designer, computer artist, photographer, production specialist, imagesetter operator, software or hardware engineer, or specialist in any of a dozen or so related fields.

At one level or another, screening offers a challenge to everyone who participates in the reproduction of an image on the printed page. Over the past few decades those in the graphic arts have usually passed screening challenges along to halftone screen designers, color trade shops, camera operators, and press operators, paying these specialists to help get the pictures right. Now, the PostScript language revolution has empowered users, developers, and engineers, who have usurped the specialists' authority. In doing so, they make decisions that profoundly influence the printing process, including halftones.

The moment you specify a graphic object that's not pure black or pure white, you require halftoning. In the process, you make critical halftoning decisions. You can't avoid the choice; if you're passive, the software decides for you by default. Your success rides on the quality of the decisions— wherever, however, and by whomever they may be made—and you are accountable for the results.

Thus, *you* are the new screening professional. The effects of your screen decisions don't become fully apparent until the ink hits the paper on the production press run. At this moment the anticipation is high: are the pictures right?

Using this book

This book will help you better understand halftones, color halftones, and Adobe Accurate Screens technology, so you can make better decisions. With the information in this book and the accompanying references, you can dig into halftones as deeply as you like. If you are familiar with hardware design, you will notice that the device descriptions in this book have been simplified and generalized. Many device design permutations could lead to interesting side trips. By ignoring these special cases, the book focuses on the essentials of the halftones rather than the details of the hardware.

The book is arranged in three parts. The first three chapters cover the fundamentals of tone and halftones, including many day-to-day realities. In case you are completely unfamiliar with halftone basics, you should brush up on this subject before beginning. Chapters Four through Seven cover general theory and introduce supercells. The discussion assumes you are comfortable with basic high school trigonometry, the essentials of PostScript software as it relates to halftones, and some basic physics. The last four chapters introduce Adobe Accurate Screens technology and offer the technical information you need if you plan to develop screens or screen sets. These chapters assume you are familiar with PostScript programming, imagesetting, and commercial printing.

The Appendices contain three PostScript language programs that have been used in the development of screen sets: a search program for first-stage screen set identification; a test page program for initial film testing; and a prototype screen filter program. The Bibliography includes extensive references, organized by topic.

This book should serve you well for several years. Chapters One through Seven cover material that should remain useful indefinitely. The final chapters discuss, among other things, Adobe Accurate Screens technology and Adobe's PixelBurst™ coprocessor, specific technologies that will remain on the PostScript language imaging scene for quite a while.

PART ONE

Fundamentals

CHAPTER ONE

Tone and Tone Relationships

Necessary to an understanding of color halftones is an understanding of black-and-white halftones, and necessary to an understanding of black-and-white halftones, is an understanding of tone.

The American photographer Ansel Adams was a master of tone. His classic black-and-white landscape photographs of the American West and Southwest compel the viewer to feel what Adams felt in his initial confrontations with the scenes. These works stand as dramatic proof that you don't need color for image impact. Tone by itself can suffice.

Free of the tyranny of color—the need for literal color truth—Adams the artist-technician was free to manipulate tone. He pushed the tone relationships in his images to the limits of believability. His talent lay in knowing how far he could provoke the viewer in black and white. Color would have gotten in his way; his tonal adventures would have shifted colors too much. Viewers would have been distressed by the "incorrectness" of the images.

Just as tone encourages experimentation, so color pulls us toward reality. Get adventuresome with color and you have announced to your viewer "Attention! I am now making art." In black and white, reality is more subjective—you can make an orange as bright as a lemon, and the odds are no one will urge you to nudge up the magenta on the orange.

This chapter touches on modern tone and value control in the prepress and printing industries. More material on the topic is listed in the Bibliography.

Tone-related terms

The language of gray is rich. Six terms in particular need to be defined: lightness, brightness, value, tone, key, and halftone. Lightness, brightness, value, and tone all describe the light reflected from the surface of an object,

3

without direct reference to the object's color. Key and halftone have more specialized meanings.

- *Lightness* represents an inherent quality of the object's surface. A white cube is lighter than a black cube, for example.

- *Brightness* is the measurable amount of light reflected under different conditions of illumination. For example, if a single light bulb illuminates three white cubes on gray velvet, the facets of the cubes vary in brightness depending on their respective distances from the light bulb, the amount of reflected light that strikes them, and the perspective of the viewer.

- *Value* is the measure of brightness of a given object in a given scene or reproduction of the scene. For example, in a photo-graph of the three white cubes arranged on gray velvet, each facet of each cube is likely to have a different value. The value of each facet depends on the nature of the photo-graph, however.

- *Tone* is not an objective, measurable characteristic. It relates to relative values and the accompanying emotional consider-ations. (Tone and value are so closely identified that many sources—Adams and this book included—speak of *tone values.*) With proper tone manipulation, you could make a photograph of the cubes on velvet feel dramatic or peaceful.

- *Key* indicates the preponderance of values in an image. A high-key image contains mostly bright values (a white egg on white china). A low-key image contains mostly dark values (a skunk in a coal bin).

- *Halftones* reproduce tone on systems where tone can't be created directly. Imagesetters, printing presses, and mono-chrome computer displays are examples of binary reproduc-tion systems that rely on halftones.

Ironically, many in the graphic arts know tone best in terms of halftones. A 30 percent tint, for example, often refers to a printed sample of a 30 percent tint, without taking into account the interplay of *two* values: the 30 percent tint and the white paper on which the tint is printed (We also rarely take into account that the printed "30 percent tint" is probably 50 percent or so, due to normal dot gain).

Light and tone

Light is perceived in one of two ways—either as direct light or as reflected light. Until about a hundred years ago, there were only a few direct light sources: sunshine, flame, lightning, the aurora borealis, stars, and some natural phosphorescence, mainly fireflies and surf. Now artificial light sources abound, and many people look at direct light sources—notably TV and computer displays—for much of the day. However, most of the natural world appears as reflected light.

To visually evaluate a scene, you rely first on tone. The myriad variations in tone allow you to judge the environment and the locations of objects within it. Tone also provides vital clues about surface characteristics (textures). In a utilitarian sense of vision, tonal content is usually all that's needed. For example, black-and-white photographs and black-and-white television consist exclusively of tone; images in these formats are rendered purely as different values of gray. (Figure 1.1.)

FIGURE 1.1
Black-and-white photographs consist of tone.

Despite the commercial attention paid to color (hue and saturation), you can usually get along without it if you have tonal (value) information. Few color-blind people notice their deficit in color perception unless they happen to be tested, and many species of animals compete well in nature with little or no color perception. Where tone—in the analytical form of brightness or value—can be described by a single number, describing color is much more complex. In the HSV color system, for example, instead of considering only value you must also consider hue and saturation. Color spaces and related discussions are outside the scope of this book; see the Bibliography.

Tonal range, tone compression, tone relationships

In the wild, if you fail to detect a predator lurking in shadows or hiding in tall grass, you become dinner. Humans, lacking acute senses of smell and hearing, need to *see* the predator. The well-developed human visual system can detect tonal subtleties in a wide range of ambient light conditions from deep shadows to bright sunlight. This corresponds to a *dynamic range* or *tonal range* of about a million to one, or six orders of magnitude from the darkest black to the whitest white. (The light of the sun is off the human tone scale.) This dynamic range isn't all available at once; we are sensitive to different areas of the range depending on the prevailing light. Our color perception varies also—all cats are gray by moonlight.

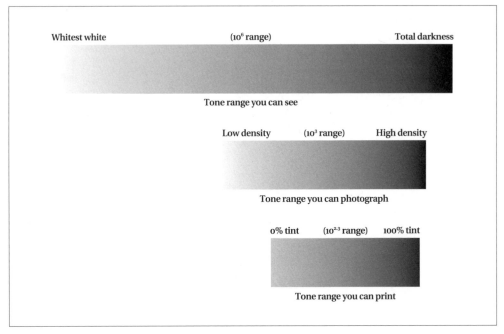

FIGURE 1.2

The eye can see a far wider range of tones than can be photographed or printed. Photography and printing compress the tonal range, but human vision adapts well to the compression.

In contrast to the wide and adaptable human range, photography can reproduce a tonal range of about three orders of magnitude, and quality commercial printing can reproduce a tonal range of about two and a half orders of magnitude (Figure 1.2). The wider the tonal range of an image reproduction system, the better its images tend to look, but nothing in commercial photography or printing comes close to rendering the full range of tone you can see.

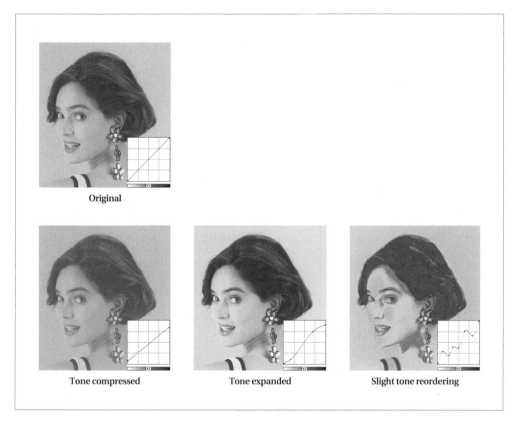

Original

Tone compressed   Tone expanded   Slight tone reordering

FIGURE 1.3
The viewer can tolerate tone compression and tone expansion well, as long as the tone relationships do not change within the image.

Nonetheless, photographs and printed images can look good, because they are seen relatively rather than absolutely. The visual system adapts quickly to prevailing conditions, immediately compensating for environmental shifts in color and tonal range. Among other things, the visual system tolerates *tone compression,* perceiving visual scenes properly so long as the *tonal relationships* in any scene appear "correct." Suppose, for example, that a photo of a sunlit scene happens to be printed on medium-gray paper with dark-gray ink. Examining the image, you perceive a sunlit scene by instantly and unconsciously evaluating value relationships in the medium-gray to dark-gray range, even though this narrow range might barely suffice to accurately describe a gray rock in the original scene. You can tolerate an enormous amount of compression in tone range, but not much variation in value relationships of familiar subjects. Juggle the value relationships carelessly and the image becomes disquieting (Figure 1.3).

Visual integration of tone

The human visual system is limited in the detail it can resolve. At a certain size threshold you no longer sense individual objects but instead *integrate* tiny objects together into average tone. The resolving limit is on the order of 1/200 to 1/300 inch, depending on the viewing circumstances. On the one hand, most people can readily distinguish the difference between laser printer output of 300 dpi and 600 dpi. On the other hand, a 133 LPI halftone screen at 45 degrees appears reasonably smooth to most people. Halftoning relies on this integration phenomenon, which allows the viewer to average millions of halftone dots into areas of perceived tone.

There is a directional component to tonal integration: within an area of tone, fine diagonal patterns are perceived slightly less well than horizontal or vertical patterns. Perhaps this is because in nature most of the significant visual edges are horizontal or vertical—trees, reeds, the horizon—and features of interest tend to interrupt these edges. Whatever the underlying reason, halftone screens look smoother at 45 degrees, where they are less apparent than at other angles, especially 0 degrees (Figure 1.4).

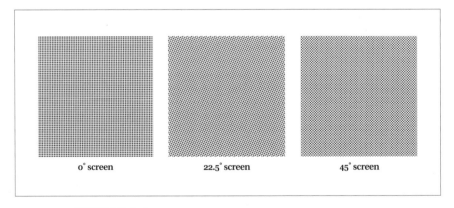

| 0° screen | 22.5° screen | 45° screen |

FIGURE 1.4

Halftone screens are most visible when oriented at 0 degrees, and least visible when oriented at 45 degrees.

Sensitivity to flaws

The more uniform the tonal background, the more apparent are minute variations or disturbances. Computer-generated artwork tends to create large, seamless areas of even tone where minor production flaws and minor abrupt tone changes stand out. Natural subjects, on the other hand, contain few areas of smooth tone except for clear sky. The natural tonal variations provide a much more forgiving background, against which the same minor production flaws and minor tone jumps are much less apparent. When these do show up they tend to appear in the sky. Ironically, adding a little tonal "noise" to an image can make it appear smoother—it slightly roughens the tonal background, camouflaging minor flaws (Figure 1.5).

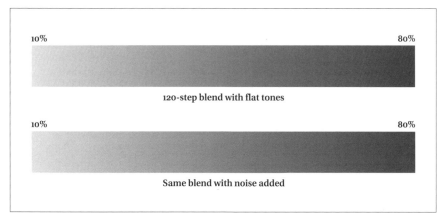

FIGURE 1.5

Adding noise to an image breaks up the smooth tonal background, making the tonal transitions appear smoother.

Tone measurement

Assume for the moment that you are observing an image in black and white. There are two questions you can ask about any given gray value within this image. First, "How gray is it in absolute terms?" Second, "How does this value relate to the other values in the image, and to the value designated as white?"

You can answer these questions with a densitometer, the basic value-measuring device. With the densitometer you sample the lightest gray value in the image—often the paper white or a clear area of film—and designate this value as zero *density units* (D). You then sample the value you wish to measure, and the densitometer assigns this sample a number on a scale that runs from zero to about six, which corresponds to extreme black. Actual densitometer measurements rarely reach six; most tone measurements fall between zero and one. Depending on the measurement protocol you follow, the design of the densitometer, and the mode of reporting, the value can be reported in density units, positive dot percent, or negative dot percent (Figure 1.6). Several types of specialized reports are possible with modern densitometers. The proper determination of tonal value is a regular and necessary step in high-quality image production.

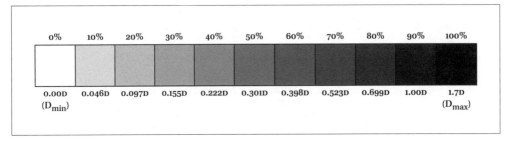

FIGURE 1.6
A densitometer assigns a number to a measured value, based on a designated zero value. Above are ideal tint densities.

Communicating tonal information

In print production you must often communicate tonal information—especially information about changes in tone value. Value changes occur in subjective image editing, color correction, color modification, and dot gain compensation. Whether you wish to add impact to a black-and-white image, precisely modify one or more color-separated components of a color image, or simply make your image look its best on a given press run, you rely on essentially the same type of tonal information.

You often want to express how an image has been changed—or will be changed—from one rendition to another. You do this by comparing before-and-after tonal data: one set of tonal information from an initial version of the image, and the other set from a subsequent version. Often the subsequent version does not yet exist.

Tone curves and tone tables

Before-and-after tonal information can be displayed as a curve in a graph or as a table (Figure 1.7). Each format has its advantages. A curve offers a quick, detailed visual interpretation of information, and can be very precise. A table is faster to construct by hand and can be quickly and accurately communicated verbally or by jotting a brief note.

For most people in the publishing world, the curve format is the familiar form: with computer software you can quickly modify tone curves and see the result on your display screen. Dot etchers and scanner operators, on the other hand, tend to work with tonal data in tabular form (at least implicitly), since they usually have just a few points of reference for any given image and must deal with these points precisely. A production supervisor will often say something like, "Bring the magenta down 5 percent in the highlights and 10 percent in the midtones."

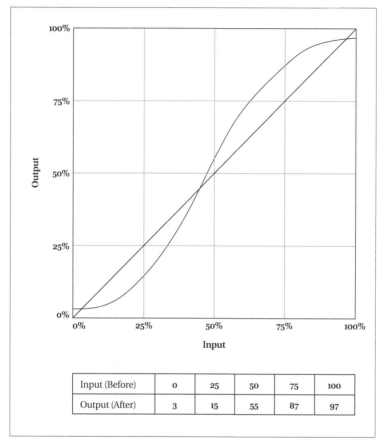

Input (Before)	0	25	50	75	100
Output (After)	3	15	55	87	97

FIGURE 1.7
A tone value graph and a tone value table, communicating the same dot-percent changes in a hypothetical image.

When necessary, graphs or tables can augment each other, but to work efficiently with other people regarding tone, color, and printing, you need to develop an intuitive sense of both formats. They represent the working language of tone in the graphic arts.

Tone graph specifics

Tone curves are graphs of before-and-after tonal data. To characterize the tone changes an image has undergone or is about to undergo, you plot the later set of tonal data on the y axis (output) against the earlier set on the x axis (input). The resulting curve describes the tonal difference between the two versions (Figure 1.8).

The data on the x and y axes are densitometer readings. These readings represent identical areas in the before and after versions of the image—either a set of reference tints or certain points of interest within the image. In actual practice, of course, these "readings" may be real or imaginary. Actual readings are used for analytical purposes when both images exist. However, a key feature of tone graphs is their ability to quickly describe *anticipated* changes, in which case the "after" readings are imaginary, representing what a set of true readings would presumably be after an intended change.

Before	0	25	50	75	100
After	0	25	50	75	100

Unmodified

Before	0	25	50	75	100
After	0	25	55	77	93

Modified

Before	0	25	50	75	100
After	0	25	55	77	93

Graph axis inverted

FIGURE 1.8

Both tone curves and tone tables are used to communicate tone value changes in prepress production. The same information can be expressed in different ways.

Over the years several different graph formats have come into common use for analyzing values in different circumstances, so you must read the axes of the tone graphs carefully. When the curve format was originally developed, densitometers were analog devices that gave readings in density units only. As a result, the traditional curve format uses density units and places low density values (image highlights) at the lower left of the graph. Modern densitometers instantly convert the logarithmic density units to more intuitive dot-percent units, so it is common now to find dot-percent notations on the axes. To complicate matters, computer software may reverse the traditional orientation of the graphs, placing the image *shadows* at the lower left. Professional graphics software sometimes offers a choice of graph formats.

In the printing industry, two tone graph formats are especially common. One format is photographic density versus dot percent, which quantifies the tone rendering from a photographic original to a halftoned replica. The other format is dot percent versus dot percent, which is used to analyze system halftone performance. Dot gain analysis and system color calibration are typical uses for this format.

Halftone Dithers

When reproducing an image, it's almost never possible to duplicate the values of the original scene. Fortunately, this isn't really necessary—
to make a believable image, all you usually need is a believable tonal representation. The eye and brain help in this effort, compensating for differences
in illumination, tonal range, and color surroundings.

Before you can arrive at a believable tonal representation, you must
establish your image-reproduction system and consider its characteristics.
There are two general categories of imaging systems: those that can reproduce acceptable tone directly and those that can't.

The first category includes systems capable of rendering *continuous tone*.
Among these are photography, television, and certain digital computer
displays of sufficient tonal resolution. (For example, a well-designed and
properly adjusted computer display with 256-gray capability can produce a
satisfying black-and-white image, especially under conditions of dim room
light.) When images are reproduced on *contone* systems such as these, halftones are not required. The reproduction of tone depends primarily on the
linearity of the system, the limits with which it produces white and black, and
the ambient light during viewing.

The second category includes systems with limited tone reproduction
capacity. These are often *binary* devices, which can reproduce only two
values that correspond to "on" and "off." In binary systems—monochrome
computer displays and commercial printing presses, among others—intermediate tones must be represented by halftones. These halftoning systems
rely on the eye and brain to integrate numerous small features to achieve the
impression of tone.

Commercial print production has historically used photographic
methods, which are inherently contone, in a distinctly binary way. This makes
sense because printing is binary—at any given location on a printed page, a
press can either put down ink or not (there is a tiny bit of mathematically
noisy gray area, which is often beneficial, as you will see later). Thus, most

prepress production steps use very high contrast films and plates. With the advent of digital imagesetters, printing is rapidly moving toward digital binary methods.

Raster devices

It usually makes sense to transmit electronic images down a single wire or over a single communication channel. In such cases the image needs to be reduced to a serial form: a series of numbers. The classic *raster* provides an orderly method for taking an image apart, converting it to serial form, transmitting it, and reassembling it at the other end of the line.

A typical raster consists of a series of horizontal scan lines. Each line is scanned in succession to gather image data or rebuild the image (Figure 2.1). The data can be analog or digital. Raster output devices—TV sets, computer monitors, and imagesetters included—zip a beam of some sort along the raster, rapidly changing the state of the beam to rebuild an image (or the impression of an image) on a screen or other light-sensitive material. TV sets, microcomputer displays, and imagesetters all represent three different categories of raster devices.

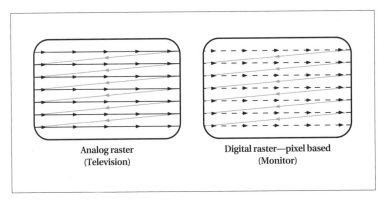

Analog raster
(Television)

Digital raster—pixel based
(Monitor)

FIGURE 2.1

An analog raster consists of horizontal scan lines. A digital raster places pixels along the scan lines.

The TV set is an analog raster device that uses an electron beam to build an image on a screen. As the TV scans the beam along its raster, it rapidly modulates the beam's intensity, which can take on any intermediate value between two extremes (the black and white on a monochrome TV set). As the electrons in the beam strike the screen surface they excite chemical phosphors, which glow in proportion to the intensity of the beam, creating a contone image. The TV set generates a complete image "frame" 30 times per second. With some help from human visual persistence, the viewer experiences the successive frames as a moving contone image. A color TV set uses three beams, one each for red, green, and blue phosphors.

Computer monitors and PostScript imagesetters are digital raster devices. They divide the raster into pixel addresses. Like the TV, a computer monitor uses an electron beam to build an image on a screen. Unlike the variable intensity of the TV set's analog beam, the intensity of the digital beam can have only one of a set of discrete values at any given pixel address. In the case of a contone digital device like a grayscale computer monitor, a rather large set of discrete values—typically 256—is needed to give the impression of truly continuous tone. In the case of a monochrome computer monitor, however, the beam has only two states—pixels are either on or off. Such a monitor is a binary raster device.

An imagesetter is also a binary raster device. But whereas a display screen uses an electron beam, the imagesetter uses a laser beam. In place of the phosphor-coated screens, the imagesetter uses photographic film. The imagesetter's very fine address grid produces an image with a higher pixel concentration, and greater detail, than the image on a display screen. In contrast to a typical TV set's resolution of 525 scan lines per frame or the typical computer monitor's addressability of 72 to 90 pixels per inch, some imagesetters have addressabilities of 3600 or more pixels per inch. Imaging engineers tend to call pixels *dots*, so imagesetter resolution is usually indicated in dots per inch (dpi).

Imagesetter film recorders are monochrome devices—pixels on processed film are either black or clear. Thus, imagesetters must play by digital halftone rules. Usually the imagesetter films are imaged as negatives, ready to use in subsequent print production steps. Of course, process color images are rendered on imagesetters as sets of four separations, each of which contains a halftoned image.

Pixels

In a digital image system the smallest image element is the *pixel*, short for *picture element*. Imagesetter output consists of binary pixels—the image is actually a very dense *bitmap*. The binary pixels in this bitmap are the conceptual and functional link between a PostScript page description language and PostScript imagesetter output.

PostScript language digital image bitmaps consist of neat rows and columns of microscopic pixels located on an *address grid* (Figure 2.2). Each of these pixels has its own unique address on the grid. The image processor uses this address to keep track of the pixel and assign it an on or off state in the image. Large high-resolution images contain billions of pixels, which places great demands on the processor.

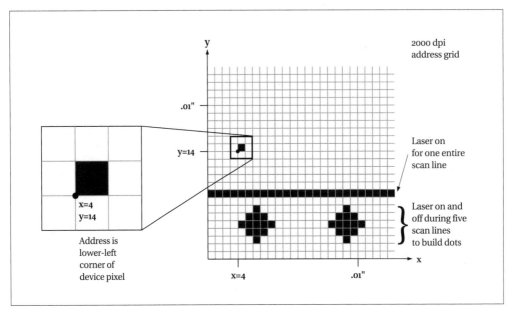

y
FIGURE 2.2

The image processor uses an address grid to keep track of the pixels.

Imagesetter pixels are usually arranged on an orthogonal grid, with x and y scales equal. In Figure 2.2 the pixels are shown as squares to represent the address grid only—actual pixels are round or slightly elliptical on film, and their diameters are increased slightly to provide complete coverage of their square grid areas. In this figure, the laser beam of the image processor scans along the x direction. To create a pixel on film, the laser is turned on briefly at the pixel's address. For contiguous pixels on a single scan line, the laser remains on. All of this happens very fast. In practice multiple laser beams are often used to scan several lines at once for more efficient imaging.

In a line-art image, a pixel is turned on if any part of the image intersects any part of the pixel's square region. For halftones, the decision to turn a pixel on or off is based on the tonal value of the image at the center of the pixel's square region.

The more pixels in a given image, the finer the address grid and the higher the *addressability.* Due to imprecise usage, the term *resolution* has become synonymous with addressability, leading to some confusion.

Resolution concerns the ability of an imaging system to reproduce fine detail; the higher the resolving power of the system, the better an image's details are reproduced. Addressability concerns the placement of pixels. As far as a digital computer is concerned, resolution and addressability are one and the same. The optical system of the output device may disagree—regardless of the *placement* of the pixels, the resolving limit is affected by the pixel *size*, which is determined by optical and photographic factors. At high resolutions on some imagesetters the pixels themselves don't change size much, they just pack together more tightly as addressability is increased. Although this improves the rendition of detail significantly, other imagesetters do better by accurately reducing the pixel size at higher addressabilities, for even finer detail. The ability to accurately render fine detail is important in imaging high-quality halftone dots.

Typical imagesetter address grids are based on square pixels, so the addressability is equivalent in the x and y directions. Some laser output devices may have different horizontal and vertical addressabilities.

Ability to image individual pixels

Every digital image reproduction system presents the halftone designer with a key question: how well can the device image individual pixels? Many displays show each pixel very clearly. Other systems, such as high-resolution imagesetters, do not. Even when a high-resolution imagesetter can image individual pixels on film, the printing process usually can't reproduce them.

This ability—or lack of ability—to reliably image individual pixels greatly affects the type of halftones that a digital image-reproduction system can use. If individual pixels can be reliably reproduced, the halftone can be based on individual pixels. Otherwise, groups of pixels must be clustered together to form larger features—halftone dots—that can be reliably reproduced.

Dithering and dither patterns

As noted earlier, halftoning takes advantage of the tendency of the eye and brain to integrate tiny features that can't be seen individually into an average tone or color. The halftoning mechanism must arrange the tiny features in such a way as to produce the most natural effect, given the constraints of the imaging system. Thus a digital halftoning system must strike a compromise among competing factors: the pixel size, the number of pixels to be averaged, and the ability of the imaging system to reproduce individual pixels.

To emulate tonal value on a digital system the pixels must be arranged in patterns. The rules for creating these patterns are very specific, and the pattern creation is known as *dithering*. A general dithering mechanism is called a dither and the specific patterns are called dither patterns. Dithers can be ordered, in which case the pattern is specific and predetermined; or disordered, in which case the pattern possesses a predetermined amount of randomness. The dither pattern in Figure 2.3 illustrates three common approaches. The clustered dot ordered dither is the basis for PostScript language halftone screens used in commercial printing. The dispersed dot ordered dither is the basis for the halftoning used on many low-resolution displays and printers. The dispersed dot diffusion dither, a disordered dither, is also used on displays. Choice of dithering approach depends strongly on the output device.

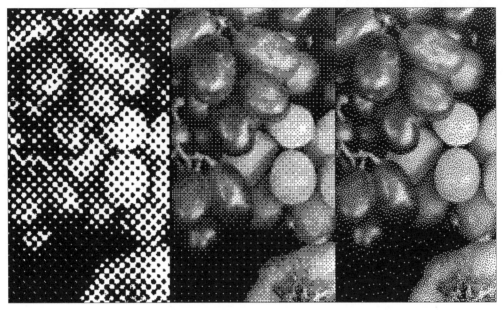

FIGURE 2.3

Dithers can be ordered or disordered. From left to right, clustered dot ordered dither, dispersed dot ordered dither, and dispersed dot diffusion dither (disordered). These images appear similar when viewed at a distance of 15-20 feet. Try it.

Digital halftoning is an active, complex, mathematically intense field in which expertise to the advanced degree level can be attained. Many different dither mechanisms are in use or under investigation. The following descriptions represent an overview; see the Bibliography if you want more information.

Halftone cells

Implicit in a dither is a region of pixels—often called the *halftone cell*—containing a specific, repeatable dither pattern. The *tonal resolution* of an ordered dither pattern depends on the number of pixels in the cell; any given dither pattern can represent a number of values equal to the number of pixels in the cell, plus one. In PostScript language halftoning systems, the tonal resolution improves with greater numbers of pixels in the cell, up to a maximum of 255 pixels. PostScript screening is based on a square halftone cell.

Within any given halftone cell in an image, a certain percentage of the pixels will be on and the rest of the pixels will be off. The percentage of pixels turned on corresponds to the tonal value this cell represents. For example, if 60 percent of the pixels in a given cell are black and the rest are white, that cell emulates an ideal 60 percent gray tint. The dither determines the distribution of these pixels. As you will see, one type of dither distributes the pixels about the cell; another type of dither clusters them together.

At any given addressability there is a trade-off between cell size and tonal resolution: the smaller the cell the smaller the number of pixels it contains, and the fewer tonal values it can represent. Thus, for the best tonal resolution—the most *gray levels*—the halftone cell should be large so as to include as many pixels as possible. On the other hand, the bigger the cell the more visible it becomes. This trade-off between gray levels and cell size is one of the classic problems of digital halftoning.

The halftone cell does not represent the minimum unit of detail in a halftoned image. If this were the case, a great deal of detail would be lost in most images. To preserve maximum detail, professional imaging systems—including PostScript imagesetters—make tonal decisions on a pixel-by-pixel basis. This preserves the available detail in the digital image, down to the size of an individual pixel on the output device.

The halftone cell forms the basis of PostScript screening, and is discussed in depth in several areas of this book.

Dispersed dot dithers

Imaging systems that reliably reproduce individual pixels can use *dispersed dot dither* halftoning. Dispersed dot dithering is familiar to many computer users due to its widespread use on computer displays. Each individual pixel on a binary display screen maintains its identity—you can take a magnifying glass and tell whether a pixel is on or off. On such a system, images tend to look best if you base the dither pattern on dispersed pixels or *dots*, hence the term *dispersed dot dither*. To give the impression of a midtone gray of 50 percent within a specific halftone cell, an average of half of the pixels within the cell can be turned on. If the screen is far enough away from a viewer's eye, the cell will appear an even 50 percent gray. Turning on other percentages of pixels gives the impression of corresponding percentages of gray (Figure 2.4).

In a dispersed dot ordered dither pattern, each halftone cell is identical in structure, with a fixed number of pixels. The dither pattern is chosen so that for each value, the cell looks as smooth as possible. The pattern details vary from one dispersed dot dither to another, and many different dispersed dot dither patterns are possible.

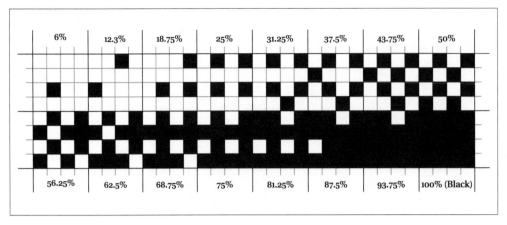

FIGURE 2.4

A 4x4 dispersed dot dither matrix can represent 17 tonal values (16 + 1). White is not shown.

Dispersed dot dithering works well as long as each pixel retains its identity. It finds much use in low-resolution output and display systems. Variations of this technique are widely used to increase the number of values that can be represented in many different kinds of halftoning.

Clustered dot dithers

As the pixel size decreases, pixels eventually become so small that the imaging system can no longer reproduce them well. For example, many of the imagesetter films used in commercial offset printing are produced at resolutions of 2400 dpi or more. The offset printing process can't reliably reproduce features of this size—its resolving limit generally lies somewhere between 0.001 and 0.002 inch—so a halftone based on a dispersed dot dither would be very difficult to control on press and could easily result in a muddy-looking mess on the printed page.

When pixels can no longer be accurately reproduced, it's necessary to turn to *clustered dot dithering*, the basis for the overwhelming majority of commercial digital halftoning for print, including PostScript imagesetter halftoning. This technique clusters the pixels in the halftone cell to form halftone dots (Figure 2.5). In contrast to individual pixels, the relatively large halftone dots can be reliably printed. Clustered dot dither patterns have a much coarser appearance than dispersed dot dither patterns, but on high-resolution output systems the halftone cells can be made small enough that the coarseness isn't objectionable.

Clustered dot dithers emulate the screen-based halftoning methods used by commercial printers since the late nineteenth century. What every commercial printer knows as halftone dots are, in a digitally-created image, clustered dot dither patterns (note how the collision of imaging terminology and printing terminology leads to two different definitions of *dot* in the same sentence).

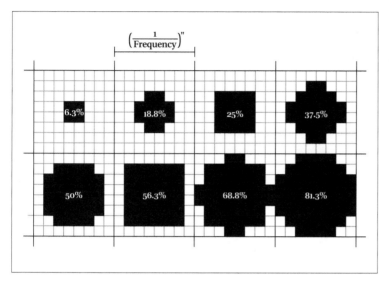

FIGURE 2.5
A halftone dot grows with increasing tone value. The percentage of the cell area the dot occupies corresponds to the tint percentage (dot percent). A halftone dot grows pixel by pixel. Dot shape is determined by a spot function.

Thus on a digital device, the halftone "screen" is the result of a computer algorithm that dictates how the pixels cluster together to form halftone dots. No physical screen is used—many skilled PostScript publishers might never have touched a contact screen—but for conceptual purposes the screen model imported from traditional printing is useful.

The early photographic halftone screens were ruled on glass. The rulings were expressed in lines per inch (LPI) or lines per centimeter, depending on the prevailing system of measurement, to indicate the distance between the screen cells, and thus the halftone dots. The screens could be freely rotated to any desired angle in the Cartesian coordinate system. The traditional halftone screen ruling and angle conventions remain, although screens and lines are no longer truly in use, and digital systems approximate the traditional screen angles. Also, some confusing terms have emerged, such as *line screen*, which can mean a dither pattern or a screen ruling, depending on context.

In PostScript screening the term *frequency* is used in place of LPI, but the two terms are used interchangeably and have virtually the same meaning in practice, as long as you are working in English measure. For example, 151.24 LPI is equivalent to a screen frequency of 151.24. This indicates a halftone screen with the halftone dots centered 1/151.24 inch apart. More precisely, it indicates a clustered dot dither pattern based on square halftone cells 1/151.24 inch on a side.

Clustered dot dither challenges

Characteristics of clustered dot dithering include halftone screen frequency, screen angle, halftone dot shape, and the growth of the halftone dot size with increasing tonal value. All of these parameters influence the appearance of a printed color halftone. Minor variations or inaccuracies can easily become visible as defects in the image. Many such variations occur in the printing process, but others can crop up in the dithering and imagesetting stages.

In clustered dot dithering you build big dots out of little dots. This invites a host of *quantization effects*, digital errors that are not simple to resolve. These can lead to visible deficiencies in the image, especially when multiple halftone screens are superimposed in process-color printing. Chief among these deficiencies are moiré patterns and tonal contouring (also called *shade-stepping*).

Considering the very large number of pixels involved, the dithering calculations for a high-resolution color image can be enormous. For an optimum result, these calculations require a computer of substantial speed and a sophisticated clustered dot dithering algorithm. It has taken several years of evolutionary development to arrive at such tools for PostScript language publishing. The current generation of PostScript language raster image processors (RIPs), are more than adequate to the task, and screening systems such as Adobe Accurate Screens software give superior clustered dot dithers.

Threshold arrays

Once a dither pattern is established, the imaging system must apply it on a pixel-by-pixel basis. To accomplish this, the system builds a *threshold array*— a table of pixel-threshold values based on the halftone cell. Each pixel within the cell is assigned a threshold value: the tonal value at which it will be turned on (Figure 2.6). To decide whether to turn the pixel on, the imaging system checks the pixel's location in the halftoned image, determines the tonal value of the image at that exact location, and compares this tonal value with the pixel's threshold value. If the tonal value exceeds the threshold value, the pixel is turned on when the image is created by the imagesetter. This represents a lot of processing, considering that a high-resolution image can have billions of pixels.

Threshold arrays can be based on a single halftone cell, or they can be larger, complex structures based on many cells (Figure 2.7). The PostScript Level 2 language provides a flexible mechanism for using threshold arrays of both types.

.52	.80	.64	.90	.44
.94	.28	.20	.32	.76
.68	.16	.04	.08	.56
.84	.36	.12	.24	.86
.48	.98	.60	.72	.40

FIGURE 2.6

One type of threshold array. This simple array assigns the threshold value for each pixel in a single 5x5 halftone cell. If the image value exceeds the value of the pixel at that location, the pixel is turned on.

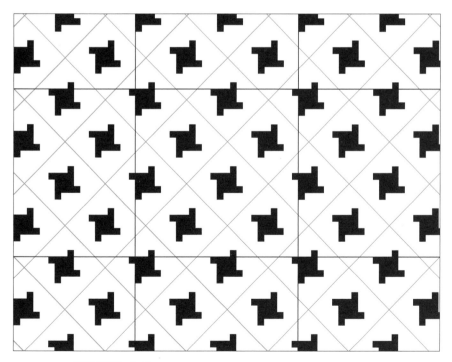

FIGURE 2.7

In this illustration a threshold array (here based on a 45-degree halftone cell) is "tiled" for more efficient halftone processing. All cells carry the same tonal value. Gray lines indicate cell boundaries; black lines indicate tile boundaries.

More to come

Since it forms the basis of PostScript screening, clustered dot dithering is discussed in the rest of this book. Chapter Four discusses moiré, which is directly influenced by both screen frequency and screen angle, and which is the initial focus in the development of screen sets for color output using Adobe Accurate Screens software. Chapter Five discusses halftone dot shape and the PostScript language spot function. Tone value relationships and the appearance of tonal smoothness enter into numerous discussions throughout Part Two and Part Three.

Halftones, Imagesetting, and Printing

Halftone dots in high-quality printing range in diameter from about 0.01 inch, for the largest possible dot in a 100 LPI screen, to about 0.001 inch, for the 3 percent highlight dot in a 200 LPI screen. Below this size the offset printing process has trouble consistently reproducing detail (features of 0.0005 inch diameter, roughly the size of a 2000 dpi pixel, have been reproduced in controlled research conditions).

Like many tiny things, halftone dots are subject to distortion in the macroscopic, human-scale, physical world. As pixels and dots journey from address grid to printed page, mathematical abstraction yields to physical machinery. During normal print production, halftone dots run a gauntlet of physical processes, each of which inevitably adds some error, jitter, or mechanical noise. These disruptions always have some effect on the final image—how much effect depends on the nature of the halftone screen, the nature of the image, and the nature of the physical processes.

This chapter concentrates on the imagesetting and printing processes, emphasizing factors that can affect the halftones. As you read, you may begin to wonder why you should bother with halftones in the face of such overwhelming odds. The good news is that the process, one way or another, usually works fairly well. That said, as a professional user of PostScript screening you need to be aware of factors that are most likely to affect your images. Armed with this knowledge, you can better pinpoint the sources of problems, and you can better appreciate the accomplishment when your images look good on press.

Due to the complexity of the topic, only the most common printing process—offset lithography—is discussed. To get the most out of the chapter, you should be familiar with offset lithography. Many printed examples of common flaws in printed halftones are available and it's a good idea to refer to them, so you're familiar with the telltale signs of common problems. See the Bibliography for sources.

PostScript imagesetters in this book

Hundreds of different output devices can generate images from PostScript language page descriptions. Many of these devices are called PostScript imagesetters. For the purposes of this book, however, a PostScript imagesetter is a high-resolution device that produces photographic film output intended for high-quality print production.

RIP and recorder

A PostScript language page description is usually generated by application software. During imagesetting, this page description is transmitted to the imagesetter in the form of an ASCII text file or binary file (the binary file offers performance efficiencies). The imagesetter has a dual task. First, it must convert the PostScript-language data stream to pixels on a raster—an electronic bitmap. Second, it must convert this bitmap from electronic to physical form.

The instrument that performs the PostScript language-to-pixel conversion is the PostScript RIP (*raster image processor*). The RIP then passes the pixel data to an output *recorder*, which contains a laser imaging engine that exposes the bitmap on photographic film.

In a laser printer, the RIP and the imaging engine are contained in a single package. In an imagesetter the RIP is often separate. This separation allows the RIP and the recorder to be matched according to the demands of the specific production site.

A typical high-resolution PostScript RIP is a special-purpose imaging computer, possibly based on a standard computing platform, with 16 megabytes or more of RAM, image-processing circuitry, one or more hard disks, various communications ports, and a video interface to the recorder. Connected to the RIP is a recorder containing a display and control panel for the operator, an interface controller for a few operator commands, and a precision laser-imaging engine designed to expose microscopic pixels on film or photographic paper. Recorders move the film or paper with a *transport mechanism*. Most transport mechanisms fall into two categories: those that feed the film along a system of rollers continuously during exposure and those that feed the film first and then hold it stationary in an internal drum during exposure. Roll-feed, or capstan, transport mechanisms tend to be less precise than internal-drum transport mechanisms. For large color halftones, internal drum recorders are preferred. In both categories, transport mechanisms of newer design offer excellent performance. Other types of transport mechanisms are also in use.

Pixels, bitmap size, and throughput

Many users of PostScript language page-description software are accustomed to thinking of imagesetters as overgrown laser printers. This assumption ignores the relative amounts of data in the respective pixel bitmaps. A 3600 dpi imagesetter bitmap has 144 times the data per square inch of a typical laser printer's 300 dpi bitmap. Halftoning and imaging speed are affected.

Intensive development efforts have dramatically improved the imaging speed of high-resolution imagesetters. Many imagesetters now process complete images considerably faster than laser printers. With a PixelBurst coprocessor or similar application-specific integrated circuits (ASICs), PostScript language image-processing speed is improved to the point that throughput is determined not by the speed of the RIP, but by the speed of the output recorder.

For the best-quality halftones, imagesetter resolutions of 2000 dpi should be considered a practical minimum. However, the very best halftones aren't always necessary. With well-designed halftone screens and special dithering algorithms, systems of lower resolution can produce excellent results in specific circumstances—newspapers, certain types of catalogs, and printing on certain uncoated paper stocks, for example.

Halftoning in the imagesetter

As discussed in Chapter Two, every pixel in a halftoned image has a threshold value associated with it. To decide whether to turn that pixel on, the RIP compares the pixel's threshold value with the image's tonal value at that location. Before any of this can happen, however, the RIP must build a threshold array and use it to assign threshold values to the individual pixels.

This process begins when the user requests a halftone screen in terms of frequency (LPI), angle, and spot function. (In PostScript Level 2 implementations you can specify a threshold array directly.) The RIP does its best to satisfy the request by calculating a threshold array for the specified screen. How closely the frequency and angle of the threshold array meet the request depends on the screening algorithm. A simple algorithm may be able to build only a few dozen possible threshold arrays. A more sophisticated algorithm (such as Adobe Accurate Screens software) offers thousands of potential threshold arrays. With thousands to choose from, the Adobe Accurate Screens threshold array is much more likely to closely (or even exactly) match the request.

The calculations necessary to build a threshold array are complex. Certain arrays require a great deal of calculation to match the user's request, and this calculation can be time-consuming, at least by computer standards. For this reason, once a threshold array is calculated an efficient RIP places the threshold array in a *screen cache*. The RIP then repeats the threshold array—which may contain many halftone cells—until the entire applicable address grid, is covered and every device pixel is assigned a threshold value. This repetition is called *tiling*. Tiling can be highly involved and proprietary.

Limited screen selection

In daily practice, few users of PostScript language-generating applications can simply specify a halftone screen and obtain that very screen on the imagesetter output. There are two completely different reasons for this, depending on the screening algorithm in use.

In the first case, with many PostScript Level 1 imagesetters the screening algorithm (RT Screening®) uses the same threshold array for every halftone cell. This restricts the potential screen frequencies and screen angles to those that can be achieved by simple sizing and rotation of a single cell. These possibilities are severely limited.

In the second case, many imagesetters that use advanced screening systems, including Adobe Accurate Screens software, choose to make only a few predetermined sets of screens available. These screens are selected within the RIP by a *screen filter* that intercepts the user's screen request in the PostScript language data stream and substitutes one screen of a *screen set*— a set of four screens designed to be used together for color printing. Screen filters protect users from specifying screens that do not work well with one another. (With most imagesetters, advanced or daring users can bypass the screen filter.) The process of finding and testing Adobe Accurate Screens screen sets is the focus of Chapters Eight through Eleven.

The imagesetting process

Virtually all PostScript language imagesetting is done on a batch basis, in which a *job* consists of a PostScript language description of a single user's page or pages. An entire job is sent to the RIP from a workstation in much the same way the same job would be sent to a laser printer (in imagesetting the print setup options are more critical). The RIP processes the job, and the recorder images the film. Software-based job queues are often employed at busy imagesetting sites to maximize throughput, provide billing information, and report jobs that fail to process properly in the RIP.

In day-to-day operation with typical jobs, a PostScript imagesetter functions largely as a "black box" with a few basic controls. Most activity centers around sending jobs to the RIP or a job queue; inserting and removing film cassettes; choosing between two or three resolution settings; occasionally setting formats, exposure levels, and film counts; processing film; and checking the quality of the output.

Considering the number of variables that enter into the imagesetting process, all imagesetter output should be carefully examined to verify that the job has produced the intended image. At the recorder's imaging engine, PostScript page descriptions cross the boundary between the electronic world and the physical world. Graphic elements that until this point existed only in abstract mathematical space or on computer displays are now rendered on film, where they are subject to vagaries of hardware, film manufacture, exposure, processing, handling, and storage. Minor physical insults can become significant problems for tiny halftone dots, especially in large even areas of synthetically created tone.

Much of the skill of high-resolution imagesetting consists of anticipating potential problems and preventing their occurrence. Well-managed imagesetting environments pay consistent attention to quality control. The following sections discuss some areas that deserve particular attention. Understanding problems that can arise during imagesetting demonstrates that a well-run imagesetting environment is far more than a glorified laser printing shop.

Flexibility and an open format help make the PostScript language powerful and universal. They also allow variations in programming style for the applications that generate the PostScript code for imagesetting jobs. Sometimes these applications interact unfavorably. In addition, many new users of these applications are unaware of normal high-resolution image-setter performance limits, and innocently construct pages that place extreme demands on the RIP. Due to the interpreted nature of the PostScript language, jobs are not compiled or otherwise checked at high resolution until they are presented to the RIP.

Thus, a few percent of jobs fail to produce the desired output due to application incompatibilities, device limits, or incorrect print setup. The situation has improved considerably due to the introduction of faster, more powerful RIPs with more forgiving device limits, but individual user education remains a primary factor in successful output. Failure to print tends to be more common at imagesetting sites that take jobs from the public. Many jobs that fail to print on the first try can be corrected and run again successfully.

The imagesetter

The physical operation of an imaging engine must be very precise to render good-looking halftones, especially at high screen frequencies. Vibrations, friction, optical misadjustments, and dust can produce a variety of odd effects, both dramatic and subtle. Many of these effects tend to show up first in halftoned areas, and tend to be distinctive in one way or another. With experience it's possible to identify the characteristic appearances of common problems, and experienced operators and service people can often do so at a glance. In other cases the problems may be hard to identify, elusive, and difficult to correct. The imagesetter operator must rely on service personnel to keep the recorder in good adjustment and smooth working order. In the event of problems, the operator should insist that servicing continue until large flat-tint halftones look smooth and uniform throughout.

Variations in laser intensity

With some imagesetters, intensity variations in the laser may cause random variation in exposure and can change the values slightly in different areas of a halftone.

Dusty or misaligned optics

A variety of optics artifacts may reveal themselves within halftones. They tend to appear as patterns that repeat at precise intervals. For example, a little dust on a spinning polygon mirror can show up as fine, regular striations parallel to the film feed direction on roll-feed imagesetters. On internal-drum units, optical misalignment can cause one side of the page to be slightly darker than the other.

Mechanical jitter

Imagesetters operate at very close tolerances. A periodic variation of a micron or two can be visible to the eye in a halftone. Every physical device has vibrations, slight though they may be, and this jitter can produce visible artifacts in halftone screens. For these devices it is often possible to design screens that don't show the jitter artifacts.

Transport maintenance and adjustment

Given the sensitivity of the eye to minor variations, consistent transport maintenance and adjustment is critical. Various artifacts can result if the transport mechanism is in need of adjustment or repair. In some cases, the artifacts suggest an electronic problem. At other times their mechanical nature is obvious. In one real-life example, a single very slightly out-of-round ball bearing took weeks to identify as the source of a halftone problem that appeared electronic.

Banding

Due to the large size of a high-resolution bitmap, few imagesetters place the bitmap in RAM all at once. Instead, they create the bitmap in sections, or *bands.* The RIP constructs these bands in a *band buffer* and sends them to the recorder as a series of broad horizontal stripes. As the film is exposed, the recorder must precisely match up the bands. If the imaging engine runs faster than the RIP can build the image, the film must stop and wait for the next band. Numerous electronic and mechanical glitches can cause minute errors in the band match-ups. These errors appear as very thin horizontal lines across the image. The imagesetter must be serviced to fix this problem.

This phenomenon is known as a band error or *banding*. The term banding is also used colloquially to describe the tonal contouring (or shade-stepping) that results from tonal quantization errors.

ROM and RIP mismatch

Electronically, the communication between the RIP and the imaging engine is managed by computer interfaces in both devices. On certain imagesetters it's possible to operate with mismatched versions of these interfaces, which can cause odd results. Occasionally a whole job images oddly or the output consists entirely of strange pixel patterns. Good management and service will avoid this problem.

Loading film improperly

Film can be loaded slightly crooked in some imagesetters. This can result in distorted output, especially right after loading.

Film

Incorrect film exposure is the leading cause of halftone value shift in image-setting. Many sites overexpose in an effort to boost the density of the dark solid areas of the film. This causes the halftone dots on the film negative to be too large, which in turn lightens the positive image created later from the negative. In extreme cases, the highlight dots can disappear entirely.

A standard procedure with each new roll of film is to establish the correct film exposure. This is done by running a test page with a set of standard halftone tints and solids, measuring these areas with a transmission densitometer, and adjusting the laser exposure as necessary until the densitometer measurements fall within specification, if possible. Modern transmission densitometers read tint percentages directly and display the values in a readout. Typical acceptable tint tolerances range from ±0.5 to ±3.0 percent of the nominal tint value at the 50 percent tint. Solid film areas are measured in density units, and should read 3.6 or better (some variation of solid density within individual negatives is acceptable, especially at densities over 4.0). As a general rule, clear areas of film should have a density reading of 0.07 or less. This reading is not critical, but a variation exceeding ±0.02 units within a negative indicates trouble with processing or fogging.

Tolerances may vary depending on the nature of the imagesetting site and the destination of the output.

In many cases it's not possible to maintain the necessary solid density and hold the tint values within tolerance. In such cases *calibration* software can be used to modify the tonal response of the imagesetter, bringing the values within tolerance.

Imagesetter film is manufactured in batches, and batch-to-batch variation is normal, especially with regard to emulsion sensitivity. Batch variation can also include assorted manufacturing defects and physical distortion due to improper storage. This can affect the position of the image on the page or the squareness of the image.

Film processing

Unstable film processing is second only to improper exposure as a cause of defective imagesetter halftones. Although this isn't an *imagesetter* problem per se, it is very much an *imagesetting* problem when it occurs. The automated processors that are universally used for imagesetter film must be regularly cleaned and adjusted, and the processing chemicals must be mixed properly and replenished at a stable rate. Development time and temperature are critical.

Small tabletop processors contain small amounts of processing chemicals. It's easy to exhaust these chemicals with a few continuous pages of film negatives, which place heavy demand on the chemistry. Imagesetting sites that generate process-color negatives require larger processors; generally bigger is better. The chemicals oxidize over time, however, so a larger processor requires more chemical replenishment, which in turn calls for more film jobs to make the large processor economical.

The test pages used for film exposure can also be used to monitor processing conditions. As with film exposure, the goal is to have densitometer readings fall within specified ranges. When it comes to film processing, it's impossible to be too vigilant. Here is a list of some specific development problems and their telltale signs.

Exhaustion of developer

In small processors especially, running a set of several film negatives at once can deplete the developer, giving a weak, washed-out look to the halftones. The individual pixels appear smaller than they should under a loupe, and in solid areas imagesetter scan lines don't overlap. Depending on the design of the processor, the development may also be uneven, with wide streaks running parallel to the direction of film travel through the processor.

Local over-development

Agitation patterns and the location of heating elements in small processors sometimes produce a local over-development that can cause broad streaks on the film, again running parallel to the direction of film travel.

Exhaustion of fixer

It's also possible to exhaust the fixing chemicals in a processor, in which case the processed film may not clear properly in unexposed areas, or may be seriously discolored. This problem is so obvious that such film will rarely find its way to a paying customer, but it has happened.

Contamination of wash water

In many geographical areas, algae thrives in processor wash water. If the wash water is contaminated with algae, the processed film can have a residue on its surface. Algicide can solve this problem, but many imagesetting sites find they can eliminate it just as effectively by swapping the transport racks for the wash water and fixer baths each time the processor is cleaned. The very slight fixer residue from the swapped rack suppresses algae in the wash water.

Flaws on rollers

The processor's rollers can age, become dirty, or develop crystals from the processing baths. Sometimes this creates tiny pinholes in the film emulsion; other times it causes streaks across the direction of film travel. To solve this problem the processor rollers must be cleaned, and often replaced.

Excessive drying temperatures in processor

If the hot-air dryer temperature is turned up too high on the processor, it can drive too much moisture from the film. This can shrink the film slightly for a day or so. The film gradually equilibrates with the ambient humidity, and in the process expands slightly. The shifting film size can create a temporary moiré pattern in the halftones.

Light leaks in film cassette

Film take-up cassettes receive hard use and can develop light leaks. These may show up as various dark spots or dark areas on the negative.

Film handling and dimensional stability

Among the four films in a typical color separation set, a dimensional variation from one negative to the next of as little as 0.001 inch can affect the color reproduction. A large piece of film can easily shift this much relative to the other pieces in the set if it's warmer or contains slightly more water than the others. The larger the film size, the more susceptible it is.

In humid conditions, film can absorb water from the atmosphere if the film supply cassette sits in the imagesetter for an extended period. The added humidity causes the film base to swell slightly, so the film dimensions may be larger on one day than another. Once exposed, processed, and stored under new humidity conditions with the original films of the separation, an isolated page can change size, which will create a moiré pattern in the final image. Thus, all films in a separation should be run at one time if possible.

Storage conditions (temperature and humidity) should be held as constant as possible to maintain consistent image size and squareness, especially for large images. The hot-air drying sections of processors should be run at a constant, and moderate, temperature. Film negatives should be delivered, stored, and handled flat—never rolled into tubes for delivery.

Film expands as it is heated. Many small light boxes run hot—once you place the film on them, the film heats up and expands. Use a cool light box if possible (they are more expensive), and otherwise allow all films in a separation to heat up together on the light box before you try to evaluate the halftones.

Proofing your color separations

If you are producing high-quality images, before committing color separation negatives to further print production, make a good color proof. This won't necessarily catch all halftone (and trapping) problems, but it will catch some of the primary culprits. It is prudent to make proofs of your commercial process-color jobs.

The offset printing process

The surprising thing about offset lithography is that it works so well, so consistently. Printers tolerate its quirky variability because lithographic printing plates can be made quickly and well at modest cost, which gives this process a strong economic advantage for medium-run quantities. As a result, offset printing satisfies the needs of hundreds of thousands of customers daily. In four-color process offset lithography, however, many things need to happen just right to achieve a top-quality outcome.

You can provide color-separated film to a printing plant in one of two ways: as loose film that must be precisely assembled into flats or as imposed film ready to use in making plates. In the latter case, unless you've worked things out in advance, the plant still needs to do some film assembly before plates can be made. Film must be precisely aligned in the making of a plate, the plate exposure must be correct for each color to be printed (often the exposure differs for one or more of the colors), and the plate itself must be processed well. On the press the images from the four plates are brought into register with one another. The press adjustments must allow for variations in the shape of the specific paper stock as it's squeezed and pulled through the press. Plate and blanket packings, blanket surface and adjustment, balance of ink and water, and inking levels are all critical also, as is the match between the paper and the ink.

The smaller the features the printing process must reproduce, the more critical all of these factors become. If there is a problem on the press run, the halftone tends to find it. The finer the halftone screen, the more critical everything becomes.

Dot gain

Dot gain occurs at the edge of inked areas—especially small areas like halftone dots—whether the edge is on the film, the printing plate, the blanket, or the paper. Many factors may cause the dots to enlarge. The more edge available, the more sensitive the screen becomes to dot gain. Thus, fine screens are more sensitive than coarse screens, since fine screens have relatively more edge. In any given screen the percentage increase in dot size goes up as the dot becomes smaller, because small dots have more edge than large dots. Statistically, the greatest amount of edge in a screen occurs in the midsize dots. This is where dot gain is most pronounced.

Dot gain is normal. Measured from negative to press sheet, it tends to run between 20 percent and 26 percent at the midtones in sheetfed offset printing. Thus, a dot that is 50 percent gray on a negative will often be 70 percent to 76 percent gray on the press sheet. By long-established custom, dot gain numbers are *added to the film values, not used as an error factor.*

Printers are sometimes reluctant to tell you their dot gain numbers. If they do provide this information, many printers will claim a dot gain far lower than 20 percent. This isn't because they are trying to deceive you, but because they measure dot gain over contract proof, not over film. In an effort to accurately emulate the look of a final press sheet, contract proofs have a substantial amount of dot gain built in. Thus, a printer often tells you the dot gain is 4 percent to 6 percent. If the typical contract proof this particular printer sees has 20 percent dot gain built in, a 5 to 6 percent gain over proof is just about right. If in doubt, ask about the printer's dot gain measurement method. If you're serious about dot gain numbers (and in high-quality circumstances you should be), occasionally run tests of your own, incorporating tint targets into your work and measuring the dot gain for yourself with a densitometer.

Printing

In printing, two types of quality-control challenges affect halftones. The first is gross errors, which require a new press run. The second challenge, much more common, is related to the lithographic process itself: the various dot gain and color-shift phenomena that are encountered and corrected, often repeatedly, on every press run.

The following are a few of the most common offset printing errors and phenomena that cause visible deficiencies in halftones. Since so many little things can vary in the course of a press run, a considerable tolerance is built into the trade customs for offset printing. Offset lithography is virtually never perfect—the goal is to find the appropriate quality ballpark and stay in it for the duration of the press run. You should be reasonable with your printer, and only demand the job be run again when errors are truly problematic.

In color work the proof forms the basis for agreement between you and the printer. Given the fast turnaround that is possible in many PostScript language publishing circumstances, some users skip the proofing stage to save time, and printers have been known to put such jobs on press. This is never recommended. In color printing, always make a proof unless you are willing to risk the entire press run.

Improper image fit

With improper image fit, one image in the press sheet shows a registration problem when all other images are in good register. This is usually caught by the printer before the job gets on press. It represents a serious error, corrected at the printer's expense, unless you have provided imposed film and approved the proofs.

Incorrect exposure during plating

Incorrect exposure during plating appears as a dot gain problem or color-shift problem in the images. Check the exposure targets on the plates if such problems can't be corrected to your satisfaction. The printer pays.

Job out of register

When a job is out of register check the edges of the image areas (assuming these are rectangular) over the entire page, as well as register targets. All should be in good alignment, with less than a halftone dot of misregister at the image edges. Achieving good register is a basic task the printer performs with each job. If you consistently encounter problems with excessive misregister when your proofs are good, find another printer.

Loose blankets

Loose blankets on an offset press can cause dot doubling, which can look like severe dot gain. It tends to happen in one color, causing a color shift. The press must be stopped, the blanket tightened, and the run brought back up to color at the printer's expense.

Incorrect press cylinder packing

Over-packed cylinders can increase the dot gain to levels higher than normal. If this occurs uniformly the color might not shift but the dot percentage will be too high, possibly leading the press operator to hold back on the ink. Tonal values will suffer. Packing is established in the press setup, so this problem is fixed at the printer's expense.

Inappropriate paper stock

Screens generally look best on coated stock. Uncoated stocks tend to allow the ink to spread out from the dot edges, increasing dot gain. Stocks with high gloss tend to slip slightly in the press, which spreads the dot out, causing slur, another type of dot gain. You and the printer should consult to make sure that the paper is appropriate for the printing you intend to perform.

Incorrect ink/water balance

Too much water can make the image look weak. On examination under a high-power loupe, the dots may have tiny whitish specks within them where microscopic water droplets held the ink out. Too little water can lead to "scumming," which slightly darkens the non-ink areas of the images. This makes the whole image look darker than it should, even though the individual dots may be the right size.

Over-inking

Press operators monitor ink densities throughout a press run, so if over-inking occurs it may appear on only a few sheets at a time and on a single stage of the press. The color will shift. Once everything else is running well, inking is the primary way to control color balance on press. It's possible to over-ink an entire job, keeping the color generally right but darkening the tones due to excessive dot gain.

The satisfaction of quality

Given all that can go wrong in imagesetting and printing, it is very satisfying to encounter sites that consistently produce excellent film and printed output for their clients. Such sites pay attention to quality control, and it pays off.

The more you work with halftones the more you will come to value good imagesetting and printing practices. It helps you get the pictures right.

Because small errors can affect a halftoned image, it pays to start with a good screen. For color work you need a well-matched set of four screens. The rest of this book covers the theory of halftone screening, especially color screening, and details a methodology for screen set development.

PART TWO

Theory

Moiré

When halftone screens are superimposed upon one another, as happens in process color printing, objectionable *moiré patterns* result. This chapter explores some practical fundamentals of moiré as it relates to screening and screen set development. Although the focus of this book is on developing screens or screen sets, if you're reading to learn more about screening in general, you can ignore the occasional references to development activities.

This chapter is light on math, striving to give you a good intuitive sense of moiré, first with simple systems of lines and grids, and then with some basic screening examples. Moiré is highly amenable to mathematical description, and several authors have explored this math in detail. The Bibliography provides ample material for exploring the theory of moiré in depth.

Adobe Accurate Screens software was originally developed to address the phenomenon of angle and frequency quantization in raster-based digital screening. Such quantization makes it difficult to obtain the exact screen angles and frequencies required in traditional screens. By making thousands of potential screens available, Adobe Accurate Screens software greatly improves your ability to find sets of screens that superimpose well without moiré.

Basics

Moiré is the interference pattern (beating) that usually occurs when two or more regular patterns are superimposed. When three or more patterns are superimposed, "secondary" moiré patterns often result as moiré patterns themselves are superimposed. The situation can become quite complex, but the distinction between primary and secondary moiré patterns is rather academic: if you can see it, it's a problem.

The regular patterns associated with moiré rarely appear in nature, but show up quite often in civilized life. Visually they are associated with the superimposition of sets of lines or grids. Acoustically they occur when similar audio tones sound together—as when two pieces of machinery hum at almost the same frequency, creating a third (beat) frequency. When this happens you hear a wow-wow-wow pattern that makes the overall sound swell and fade periodically. The frequency of the wow pattern equals the *difference* between the two audio frequencies.

Varying frequency with parallel lines

Parallel lines offer a good place to start learning about moiré. Once the line examples are clear, it's easy to move on to grids, which form the basis for half-tone screens. (In this book, some device-dependent moiré patterns may develop due to quantization effects as the examples are imaged on a digital raster. The lower the device resolution, the more apparent this moiré will be.)

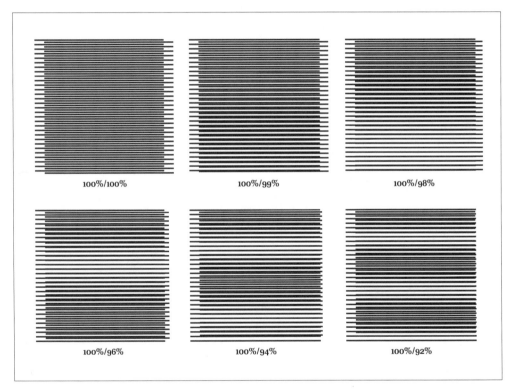

100%/100%   100%/99%   100%/98%

100%/96%   100%/94%   100%/92%

FIGURE 4.1
Varying the frequency of one of two sets of parallel lines.

A simple and informative moiré example is the venetian blind case of two sets of parallel lines. In Figure 4.1, two sets of parallel lines are superimposed, with the second set varying in size from 100 percent to 92 percent of the first set. Naturally, this size variation affects the frequency of the lines in the second set. In the 92 percent example, a regular moiré pattern is evident as horizontal bands of light and dark. In typical interference patterns, the larger pattern results from the alternating cancellation and reinforcement of one of the underlying patterns by the other. In Figure 4.1, the cancellation and reinforcement between the two underlying sets of lines appears as alternating bands with even spacing.

Moiré frequency and period

There is a correlation between the frequencies—the lines per inch—of the underlying patterns and the frequency of the resulting moiré pattern. The moiré *period* (the distance over which the moiré pattern repeats, sometimes called moiré *length*) is related to the difference in frequency between the underlying parallel-line patterns, regardless of the frequencies involved:

$$\text{Moiré frequency} = |f_{set1} - f_{set2}|$$

where f is the parallel line frequency in any unit of measure, and the vertical lines denote absolute value. The moiré period is the inverse of the moiré frequency:

$$\text{Moiré period} = \frac{1}{|f_{set1} - f_{set2}|}$$

For example, in Figure 4.1 the 100 percent set of lines has a frequency of 21 lines per inch (LPI). The 92 percent set of lines has a frequency of 0.92×21 or 19.3 LPI. The frequency difference between the two sets is 1.7 LPI, so the moiré frequency is 1.7 LPI, and the moiré period is 1/1.7 or 0.59 inch.

To have *no* moiré in the case of two superimposed sets of parallel lines, the moiré frequency must be zero. In other words, each of the two sets of lines must have the same frequency. If the difference in frequency is small enough, however, the moiré frequency is very low. Correspondingly, the moiré period is very long—so long that the moiré pattern is not evident.

Varying angle with parallel lines

Figure 4.2 illustrates a case where the frequency of the sets of parallel lines does not vary, but the angle between them does. Two sets of parallel lines of equal frequency are superimposed at various angular offsets from 0 to 90 degrees. A moiré pattern with a long period immediately emerges at low angles of rotation. The moiré period becomes smaller with increased angular offset. By a 45-degree offset the moiré period is short enough that the eye no longer perceives a moiré pattern, and the appearance becomes essentially uniform for the rest of the angular offsets up to a 90-degree offset. Despite the uniform appearance, the period continues to shorten a bit more, until at a 90-degree offset the two sets of lines form a quadratic grid with a completely uniform structure.

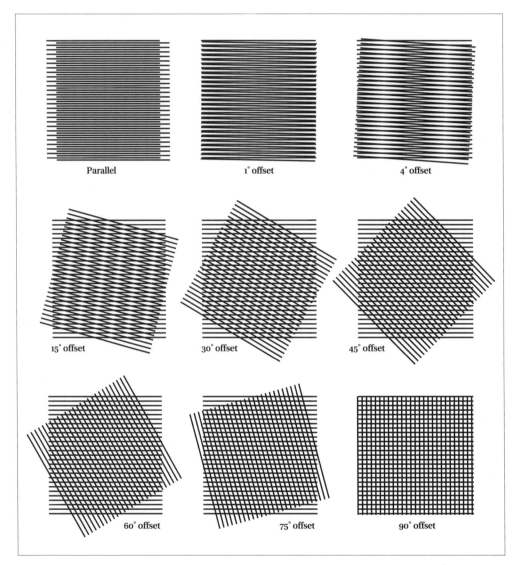

FIGURE 4.2
Systems of parallel lines with varying angular offsets.

Were the rotation to continue, the same moiré patterns would simply occur in the reverse order until the lines were perfectly parallel again at 180-degree offset.

Notice that the moiré pattern itself has an angle. This angle falls between the angles of the two underlying sets of lines. If one of the underlying sets of lines stays at 0 degrees—as is the case here—the moiré pattern has an angle equal to half the rotation of the other underlying set of lines. This boils down to $\alpha°/2$, where $\alpha°$ is the offset angle of the second set of lines. In contrast to the Figure 4.1 case with parallel lines of varying frequency, where the moiré frequency is independent of the actual frequencies and simply equals their difference, with the angled sets of lines the moiré frequency increases along with that of the lines. When both sets of lines have the same frequency (LPI), the moiré frequency is:

$$\text{Moiré frequency} = \frac{LPI}{2\sin\left(\frac{\alpha}{2}\right)}$$

When the angles of the two sets of lines are the same—0-degrees offset—no moiré is present because the sine of 0 degrees is zero. The moiré frequency is infinitely large. At the other extreme—90-degrees offset—90 degrees divided by 2 is 45 degrees, and the sine of 45 degrees is 0.707. Thus the moiré frequency is LPI/1.414. Recall that 1.414 is the square root of 2, and is also the length of the diagonal of a square whose side is 1. At 90-degrees offset, the moiré period coincides with the corners of the grid pattern formed by the two parallel line patterns when one of them is offset by 90 degrees. The moiré is not apparent.

Unstable and stable moiré-free states

In the previous examples, there are two types of moiré-free states: unstable and stable. An unstable state remains free of visible moiré, but exists on a knife edge—the slightest disturbance in the system results in the development of a pronounced moiré pattern. Such an unstable state occurs in the case of exactly parallel lines of exactly equal frequency. Under this tenuous condition there is no moiré pattern—but as the parallel lines become more finely spaced, achieving and maintaining the perfectly parallel condition becomes increasingly difficult in the physical world.

A stable moiré-free state occurs at the 90-degree offset in Figure 4.2, where there actually is a moiré pattern, but it's not evident since it lies within the grid structure. In this case, the two sets of lines can tolerate errors of up to about 45 degrees from the 90-degree offset condition before a significant moiré pattern appears.

Varying frequency with two grids

In Figure 4.3, two quadratic grids are superimposed, with one of the grids varying in size. Notice that the moiré pattern is now quadratic also. The 100 percent to 100 percent case represents an unstable moiré-free state.

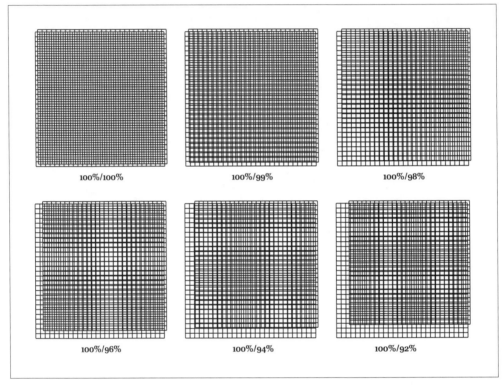

FIGURE 4.3
Varying the frequency of a set of two grids.

Two grids, varying angle

Figure 4.4 shows two identical quadratic grids superimposed as one of them rotates clockwise through 90 degrees. This situation is analogous to the rotation of two sets of parallel lines, with one key exception—the grids exhaust their superimposition possibilities over a 90-degree offset range, not over a 180-degree range like the parallel lines. For the two grids the 0-degree and 90-degree offset conditions represent an unstable moiré-free state, and the 45-degree offset represents a stable moiré-free state.

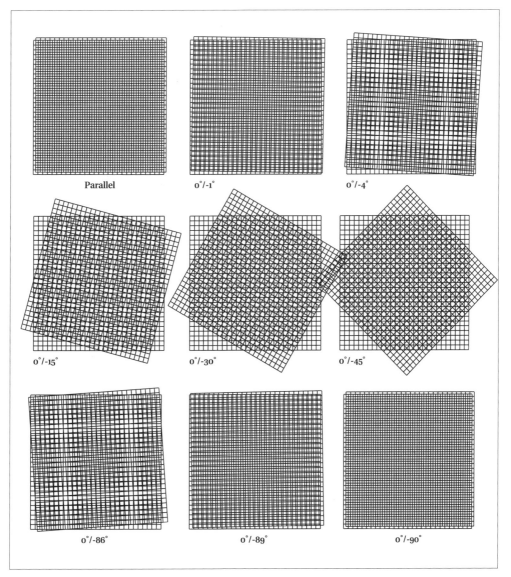

FIGURE 4.4
Varying the angular displacement of two grids.

Notice the interesting rosette-like structures evident in the 30-degree and 45-degree offset examples.

Superimposition of three grids

In Figure 4.5, three quadratic grids, each of 20 LPI, are superimposed with exactly 30-degree offsets. The grids are positioned at 0 degrees, 30 degrees, and 60 degrees, and the resulting moiré pattern shows a well-defined rosette structure. In Figure 4.6, the 60 degree screen has been shifted by about 0.8 of a grid square. Notice how the form of the rosettes has shifted from filled centers to clear centers, and how the overall structure of the clear-center pattern appears more open.

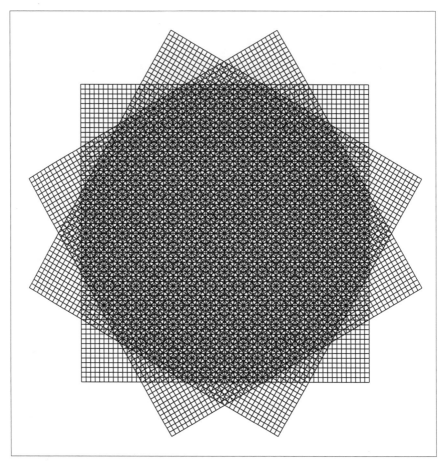

FIGURE 4.5
Offsetting three concentric, equal-frequency grids by 30 degrees.

The rosette structures in Figures 4.5 and 4.6 represent an unstable moiré-free state. The rosettes themselves are moiré patterns. In these cases the rosettes are consistent across the sets of superimposed grids. In Figure 4.7, however, the angle of the 30-degree grid has been changed by 2 degrees, to 32 degrees. Now an obvious moiré pattern has developed; it manifests itself by a well-defined periodic shifting between the filled-center and clear-center patterns, and is itself quadratic. It is analogous to the moiré patterns that emerge in four-color printing when screen angles or screen frequencies are inconsistent in superimposed screens. This same basic moiré pattern occurs whether caused by the angles, frequencies, or both.

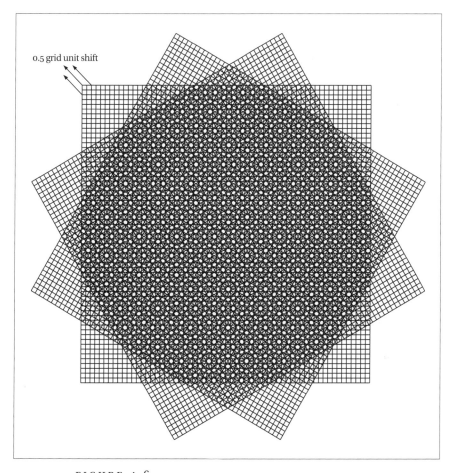

0.5 grid unit shift

FIGURE 4.6
Shifting one of Figure 4.5's grids by 0.5 of a grid square produces a clear-centered pattern.

Dot screens derived from grids

So far this chapter has dealt with parallel lines and grids. Halftone screens are simply a specialized case of grids. If you take a quadratic grid and show only the grid intersection points, you produce a quadratic halftone screen pattern. Mathematically, this quadratic screen performs similarly to the quadratic grid. Moiré patterns analogous to those that emerge with the superimposition of grids emerge with the superimposition of screens derived from the grids.

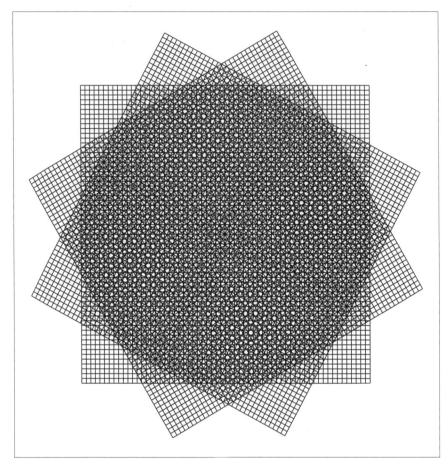

FIGURE 4.7
Rotating one of three, 30-degree offset, equal-frequency grids by 2 degrees.

Classic 3-screen rosettes and color shift

Figure 4.8 shows three screens of equal frequency arrayed in the classic 15-, 45-, 75-degree orientation to produce the classic rosette pattern. The pattern is shown in its two extremes: clear-centered and dot-centered, analogous to the clear- and filled-centered rosette patterns in Figures 4.5, 4.6, and 4.7.

Also shown in Figure 4.8 is a moiré pattern with several definable intermediate patterns between the clear- and dot-centered extremes. All of these intermediate patterns are simply the result of minute positional variations in the three screens. Recall from Figure 4.6 that it required a grid shift of less than a single grid square (here a single dot) to move from a filled-centered moiré pattern to a clear-centered moiré pattern.

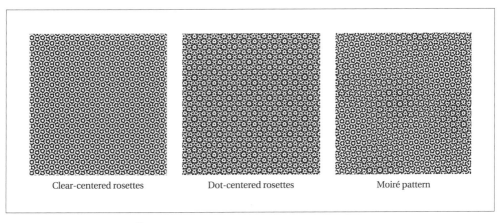

Clear-centered rosettes   Dot-centered rosettes   Moiré pattern

FIGURE 4.8
Patterns produced by various arrangements of three screens of equal frequency.

The critical difference between the clear-centered and dot-centered rosettes lies in the *superimposition of the individual screen dots* of the screens. A slight shift in the position of just one of the screens changes the rosette form. With the dot-centered form, however, the individual screen dots tend to fall on top of one another more than they do in other rosette forms. Since printing inks do not behave in an ideal manner, dot-on-dot printing produces a slightly different color than dot-beside-dot printing for dots of the same size. Consequently, an area of paper printed with dot-centered rosettes can show a slight color shift relative to a similar area printed with clear-centered rosettes. If the color being printed falls in an appropriate range and the two types of rosettes are present in close proximity—as they are in a medium frequency moiré pattern—the color shifts as the rosette forms shift. You see the color shifts as a moiré.

Screen misalignment and moiré period

In Figure 4.7, a change in the angle of one of the grids produced a moiré pattern visible as a periodic shifting between rosette forms. The same thing happens with screens. Due to the low frequency (20 LPI) of the grids in Figure 4.7, a 2-degree change in angle was needed to clearly illustrate the shifting within the dimensions of the figure; the moiré pattern in Figure 4.7 has a period of about 1.4 inches. The geometry of such systems can be linearly scaled. Thus, a similar 2-degree angle error in a 150 LPI system would produce a moiré with a period of about 0.19 inches. (A 150 LPI system is 0.133 times the scale of a 20 LPI system, and 0.133 times 1.4 is 0.187.)

An error of 2 degrees is enormous by commercial printing standards. As every student of print production knows, it takes only a very slight error in screen angle or screen LPI to produce a highly objectionable moiré pattern. This situation exists because *the classic rosette pattern relies on an unstable moiré-free state.* Like the simpler unstable states illustrated earlier in this chapter, the classic rosette is highly vulnerable to slight perturbations.

In the real world of commercial color printing, numerous factors can result in minor errors of angle or frequency in the superimposed process-color screens. If the colors being printed are such that a significant color shift occurs between dot-centered and clear-centered rosettes, a moiré pattern appears.

Desirability of clear-centered rosettes

Since clear-centered rosettes offer slightly better color performance and maintain better picture detail in deep shadow areas, the printing trade prefers them. The least favored structure is the dot-centered rosette, since the color shifting hits a maximum as the dots move on top of one another.

Maintaining a perfectly consistent rosette structure throughout a press run is exceedingly difficult, since the slightest misregistration causes the structures to shift in form. Thus, since the clear-centered and dot-centered rosette forms lie at the extremes of the moiré pattern, and since the screen errors are often very slight, it is considered good practice in the printing trade to start with clear-centered rosettes. This gives the greatest allowance for error as production proceeds.

Rosette consistency

In their visual checks, printers often use the distance between the centers of the dots in a halftone screen as a reference. In principle, a registration error of about 0.5 times this distance can occur before dot-centered structures show up on the press sheet. This degree of error is tolerated in most color printing. *Since a certain amount of shift is highly likely during printing, the exact rosette form is less important than form consistency.*

Thus it's important that rosette structures are as constant as possible on the film and free of built-in shift. This allows the stripper to build the rosette (adjust the position of the films on the stripping table so they create a clear-centered rosette on the press sheet). Even in cases where dot-centered rosettes end up on the press sheet, this won't cause an overwhelming problem if the rosettes are consistently dot-centered, because visible color shift will be absent or slight.

Four screens and 15-degree moiré

With three screens and 90 degrees to work with in a quadratic system, the screens fit nicely with 30-degree offsets. The four-color process, however, puts the printer in a quandary—how can one accommodate the fourth screen without encountering a visible moiré? The simple answer: you can't avoid a moiré, but you can minimize its visibility.

In traditional color screening, where all four screens have the same frequency, the least detrimental placement for the fourth screen is between two other screens, offset 15 degrees from each of them. A characteristic 15 -degree moiré pattern results.

FIGURE 4.9
Two equal-frequency grids with a 15-degree offset.

Figure 4.9 shows two equal-frequency grids superimposed with an angular offset of 15 degrees. A crosshatch moiré pattern is evident. Figure 4.10 shows two equal-frequency *screens* superimposed with a 15-degree offset. The crosshatch pattern has transformed into a classic linen-pattern 15-degree moiré, which has a period of about four times the period of the underlying screens.

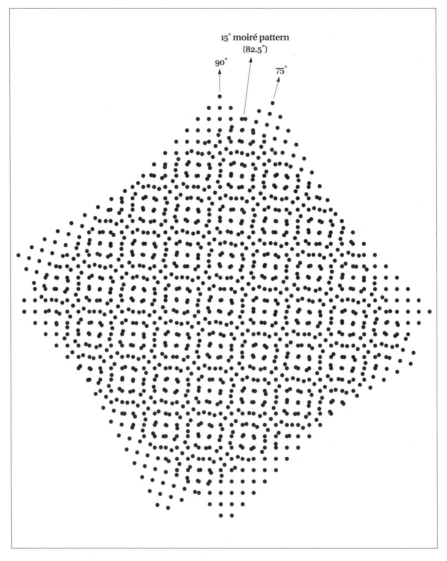

FIGURE 4.10

Two equal-frequency screens with a 15-degree offset. The moiré pattern is angled between the screens. (Notice that it's the alignment of the dots and not the border of the screen that determines the screen angle.)

This 15-degree moiré is most noticeable when the values in the respective screens are roughly 30 percent of full color. It's the most common moiré encountered in traditional four-color commercial printing, because it's always present regardless of the screens' positional accuracy. Certain colors—ones that employ screens with 15-degree offset—tend to develop this moiré (Figure 4.11).

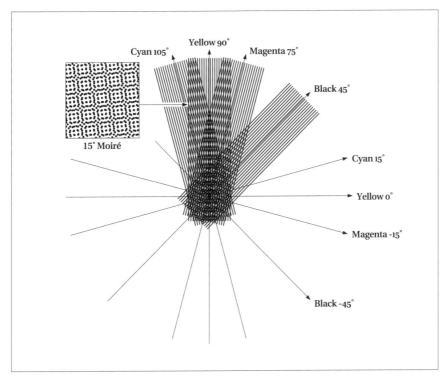

FIGURE 4.11

The traditional screen assignments call for four screens of equal frequency.
This creates 15-degree moiré patterns between yellow and cyan, and yellow
and magenta.

Traditional screen assignments

The goal with commercial printing is to make the halftone screens as unobtrusive as possible. Various standard screen assignments have emerged over
the years to accomplish this in the traditional case where all four screens have
the same frequency.

Usually the darkest ink is printed with a 45-degree screen, since the least
visible screen orientation is 45 degrees. The other three process inks are
assigned angles relative to 45 degrees, roughly in proportion to their visibility.

The typical assignment scheme is illustrated in Figure 4.12. Since black is
the darkest ink, black is assigned 45 degrees when significant screened
amounts of it are present in an image. Cyan and magenta are assigned 15
degrees and –15 degrees (equivalent to 75 degrees) interchangeably, since
these angles are equally visible. Yellow, the lightest color, is assigned between
the cyan and magenta at 0 degrees, a highly visible orientation but one that
rarely matters, given the lightness of yellow in comparison to the generally
white paper stock.

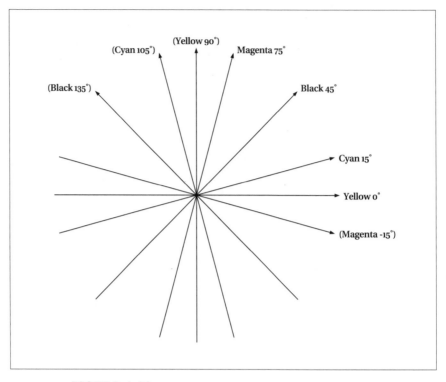

FIGURE 4.12

Typical screen-angle assignments. Assignments may be swapped for various reasons. The angles in parentheses, although equivalent for each screen, are specified less often.

Keep in mind as you examine Figure 4.12 that there are only 90 degrees to work with in a quadratic system, so any given angular assignment repeats itself every 90 degrees. For example, the 15-degree screen is equivalent to a 105-degree screen, and the 75-degree screen is equivalent to a –15-degree screen. The 0-degree screen is equivalent to a 90-degree screen, and so forth. Thus, the 15- and 75-degree screens are mirror images of each other across the horizontal and vertical axes, something that becomes important when you are imaging on a raster.

Swapping screens

Many permutations of the standard screen assignments are possible, and, depending on the image, the typical assignments are often *swapped* by prepress houses. In the most common swap, an image with important flesh tone and only a small amount of black screen is often printed with magenta at 45 degrees and black at 75 degrees (Figure 4.13). Such a swap accomplishes two things. First, it assigns the dominant color—magenta in this case—to

45 degrees for minimum visibility. Second, it removes the standard 15-degree relationship between magenta and yellow, and replaces it with a 15-degree relationship between black and yellow.

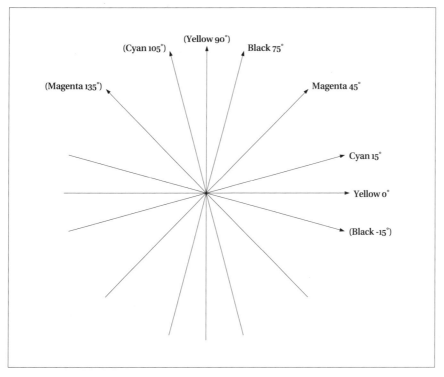

FIGURE 4.13
With the traditional screen assignments, screen positions can be swapped to remove the most problematic 15-degree moiré pattern. The swap depends on the nature of the image. Here the black and magenta screen have been swapped.

With the 15-degree relationship between magenta and yellow removed, there is far less risk of a 15-degree moiré pattern emerging in the light pinks and oranges. Many flesh tones are predominantly light pink or orange, where the simultaneous use of yellow and magenta gives a color that tends to show moiré. Without this screen swap, people in the image can develop a mesh pattern in the skin tones of about four times the halftone screen frequency.

The occurrence of such moirés depends very much on the press work, so the moirés may come and go in the course of a press run. This presents a serious quality-control problem in commercial printing. Various other 15-degree moirés can emerge also.

The black-for-magenta swap described here substitutes a black and yellow relationship that rarely causes much trouble; it appears in certain dark greens. It does, however, leave the 15-degree cyan and yellow relationship in place, making light greens susceptible to 15-degree moirés. Thus, it's challenging to print moiré-free images that contain flesh tones and light greens when all four halftone screens have the same frequency. Moiré patterns are easiest to see when the colors that contain them are uniform, so one possibility is to make the colors slightly random, such as happens with green grass or green stucco. In most publications, for example, light pinks and light greens tend not to appear together in photographs, and when they do, one of them is often textured. In cases where they appear together but no texturing is possible, a 15-degree moiré pattern is often visible if you look closely.

Eliminating visible 15-degree moiré

The traditional screen assignments assume that all four screens have the same frequency. This assumption is perfectly reasonable in a case where the same physical screen is used to create color separations—the screen is simply rotated to different angles to create the halftoned negatives.

Digital screening is much more flexible. Depending on the screening algorithms, many screens of varying frequencies are available to combine into screen sets. Thus, in digital screening another approach has developed that greatly reduces the apparent 15-degree moiré: the frequency of the yellow screen at 0 degrees is changed. This does not eliminate the 15-degree moiré, but changes its character in such a way that it becomes less apparent, and no screen swapping is needed to avoid it.

The frequency of the yellow screen can increase or decrease. In general, an increase to approximately 108 percent of the frequency of the other three screens produces a visually moiré-free screen set.

Complementary variations

On a raster system, digital screens are symmetrical about the x and y axes. In the typical case where a screen is based on a square grid, the screen itself repeats every 90 degrees. Thus, if you ignore any asymmetries of the halftone dots themselves, placing a screen at 15 degrees is equivalent to placing it at 105 degrees. Also, screens at 75 degrees and 105 degrees are mirror images of one another.

You've seen that the yellow screen can usually be removed from consideration in building the classic rosette. This leaves three screens at 105 (or 15) degrees, 45 degrees, and 75 (or –15) degrees.

The 105- and 75-degree screens are mirror images of one another across the y axis (or if you prefer, these same screens at 15 and –15 degrees are mirror images of one another across the x axis). For reasons discussed in Chapter Six, it's difficult to achieve angles exactly 15 degrees off an axis in a digital system, so there is almost always a minor error in the 15- and 75-degree angles. The screens at 15 and 75 degrees have the same frequency, however, since they are mirror images of one another.

In addition, due to digital raster considerations the frequency of the 15- and 75-degree screens almost always varies slightly from the frequency of the 45-degree screen. It would seem that these variations dictate that digital systems always have some moiré present in their color screen sets. *Fortunately, however, these angle and frequency variations can sometimes compensate for one another, giving a moiré-free state and ideal rosettes despite the fact that the digital screens differ from the traditional analog ones.*

High expectations

Digital screening has progressed rapidly in recent years. The current expectation for digital screening is for no visible moiré in sets of four-color screens and no detectable rosette shift. Since rosette shift *is* moiré, this means that the current expectation is for no moiré. Once print production begins, however, some error always creeps in. Much testing remains to be done over the coming years to establish screening systems that live up to the new moiré-free expectations.

Halftone Dot Shape and Spot Functions

Typical discussions of PostScript language halftoning concentrate on screen angles, frequency, and moiré patterns. Dot shape is mentioned in passing, if at all. True, when moiré is present it's difficult to concentrate on much else, but once problematic moirés are designed out of a screening system, dot shape becomes a key factor in screen function and appearance.

Dot shape is governed by the PostScript language spot function. Besides using the spot function in PostScript code, you can assign spot functions in Adobe Photoshop™, various other application programs, and PostScript Printer Definition (PPD) files. This chapter presents several spot functions representing dot shapes now used in color print production.

In PostScript Level 2, user-defined threshold arrays can be used in place of a spot function. This is useful in various situations. For example, you may use a dispersed dot ordered dither pattern or a nonsquare halftone cell. However, such user-defined threshold arrays cannot be used with Adobe Accurate Screens software.

Refer to the *PostScript Language Reference Manual* for the fundamentals of setting screens, the operation of spot functions, and the halftone cell coordinate system.

Basics

As discussed in detail in the *PostScript Language Reference Manual*, spot functions assume a square halftone cell with its own special coordinate system. In the cell coordinate system, the origin is in the middle of the cell and the four corners of the cell correspond to x and y coordinates of –1,–1 for the lower left; 1,–1 for the lower right; 1,1 for the upper right; and –1,1 for the upper left. Thus each pixel address within the cell is given by a set of coordinates than ranges between –1 and 1. Given these coordinates, all spot functions return a single number between –1 and 1.

This number is the pixel order number. It determines the pixel's ordering in the halftone cell, and thus (after some internal calculations) its threshold value in the threshold array. The threshold-array values range from 0 to 255.

Criteria for dot shape

Figure 5.1 illustrates a round dot in a 0 to 100 percent gray fountain. The spot function that produced the dot appears below the fountain. Notice that the dot grows evenly as tonal values become darker. Since the round dot has a symmetrical, unchanging shape, only its size changes over the tone range—not it's shape.

Why not just use a round dot and be done with it? It turns out that the round dot, like virtually all simple dots, has strengths and weaknesses in high-quality print production. The round dot, for example, exhibits poor behavior in the shadow region.

An ideal dot shape:

- Minimizes the effects of dot gain throughout the tonal range.
- Holds the ink reliably at smallest size (2 to 3 percent highlight dots) to provide the best possible foothold for the ink.
- Delivers the desired behavior in the tonal zone where the dots join.
- Resists the tendency to fill prematurely with ink at large size (80 to 93 percent shadow dots).

No one dot shape meets all four of these criteria well, although there are some reasonable compromises. In most cases, the best dot for a given task uses a variety of shapes. Such dots are often called *composite* or *composed* dots in the color trade.

Dot gain and dot shape

As a general rule, compact dots show the best dot gain behavior. The most compact dot is a round dot, which performs well in terms of dot gain. The simple circle shape is part of many spot functions.

Since different dot shapes have differing amounts of edge and show different dot gain behavior, to avoid visible tone jumps, it's advisable to change gently from one dot shape to another.

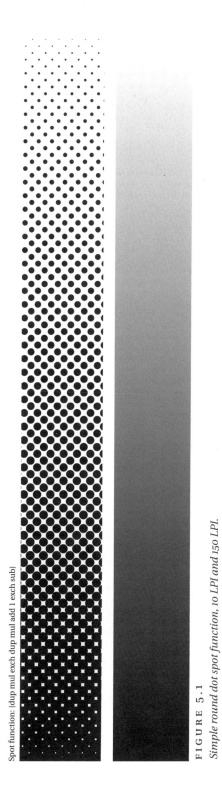

Spot function: {dup mul exch dup mul add 1 exch sub}

FIGURE 5.1

Simple round dot spot function, 10 LPI and 150 LPI.

Spot function: {abs exch abs 2 copy add 1 gt {1 sub dup mul exch 1 sub dup mul add 1 sub} {dup mul exch dup mul add 1 exch sub} ifelse }

FIGURE 5.2

Euclidean composite dot spot function, 10 LPI and 150 LPI.

Spot function: {abs exch abs 2 copy add .75 le {dup mul exch dup mul add 1 exch sub} {2 copy add 1.25 le {.85 mul add 1 exch sub} {1 sub dup mul exch 1 sub dup mul add 1 sub} ifelse } ifelse }

FIGURE 5.3
Diamond dot spot function, 10 LPI and 150 LPI.

Spot function: {dup mul exch dup mul add 1 sub }

FIGURE 5.4
Inverted round dot spot function, 10 LPI and 150 LPI.

66

Spot function: {dup mul .9 mul exch dup mul add 1 sub }

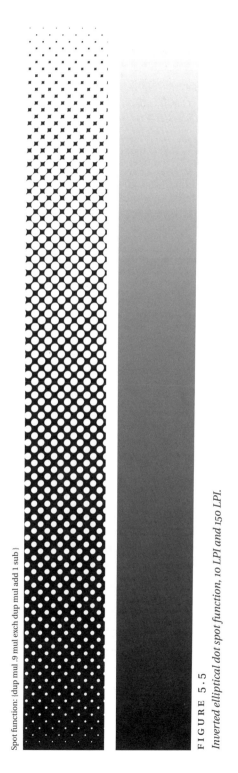

F I G U R E 5 . 5
Inverted elliptical dot spot function, 10 LPI and 150 LPI.

Spot function: {abs exch abs .8 mul add 2 div}

F I G U R E 5 . 6
Rhomboid dot spot function, 10 LPI and 150 LPI.

Providing a foothold in the highlights

Many printing inks are granular due to the ground pigments they contain. These inks have a threshold below which they don't adhere well to the paper. At resolutions above roughly 2000 dpi, the smallest highlight dots—one or two pixels in size—fall below this threshold and don't print reliably. In addition, blanket abrasion can rub the small highlight dots off an offset printing plate. For these reasons, the finer the screen (the higher the frequency), the smaller the highlight dots and the more difficult it is to print them well.

Compact dots perform well at small sizes, so in the highlights, round dots offer an advantage.

Dot join

The round dots' advantage disappears abruptly as the dots become larger. Now the symmetry and compactness of the dot lead to an abrupt change in character, as the dot touches its neighbors on four sides. On film this occurs at 78.5 percent gray.

Other dot shapes exhibit even more pronounced joining behavior. One of these is the Euclidean composite dot (Figure 5.2). This symmetrical dot passes through a perfect checkerboard pattern at 50 percent gray, touching its neighbors at four points at once.

Such joins are visible as abrupt tone jumps in areas of tonal transition, as can be seen in the 150 LPI fountain in Figure 5.2. At the point where the screen forms a checkerboard pattern you should be able to see a jump in tone. Tone jumps are highly inking-dependent. Depending on the state of the printing press when Figure 5.2 was printed for your copy of this book, you may have to look closely to see the jump or it may be obvious. Such jumps tend to be worse in areas of rapid tone transition, such as short fountains (Figure 5.7). Tone jump behavior can be useful for certain images when you want a sharp tone break, but most images look best with smooth tonal transitions.

To make smooth tonal transitions, the dots need to be made asymmetrical so they won't touch on four sides at once. In practice this usually means the use of elliptical or diamond-shaped (rhomboid) dots (Figures 5.3 and 5.6). With biaxial symmetry instead of quadriaxial symmetry, the dots touch first at their long axis, and later in the tone range at their short axis. By adjusting the spot function, you can easily vary the relative lengths of the axes to adjust the width of the tone region over which the joining occurs (Figure 5.8). Press work is more critical for elliptical and rhomboid dots, which are more sensitive to slur than symmetrical dots.

Shadow behavior

On a printing press, once the dots have joined, the remaining white area becomes susceptible to "plugging" with ink. The simple round dot performs poorly in the shadows, since the remaining white area contains cusps that readily fill with ink. These areas have a great deal of edge compared to their area. This encourages dot gain.

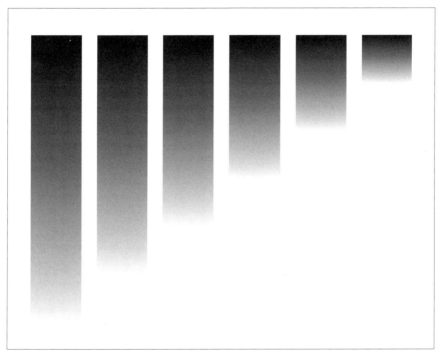

FIGURE 5.7

Dot join effect due to checkerboard pattern at 50 percent gray. The effect is more pronounced in short fountains.

Optimum performance in the shadow region calls for *inverted* round dots (Figure 5.4). Inverting the circles minimizes the edge and shadow performance improves. With all dot shapes the shadows are vulnerable to plugging, and press operators must take this into account when printing images with important shadow detail.

Exploring spot functions

Writing spot functions requires you to use both sides of your brain. If you experiment, you can often obtain equivalent results with far less code one way than another. Spot function intuition can't really be taught—it's best to start experimenting with spot functions, beginning at some known point and exploring new ground on your own.

In the following discussion, keep in mind that the pixel ordering goes in one direction only. Once a pixel is turned on in a halftone cell, it stays on throughout the development of the dot.

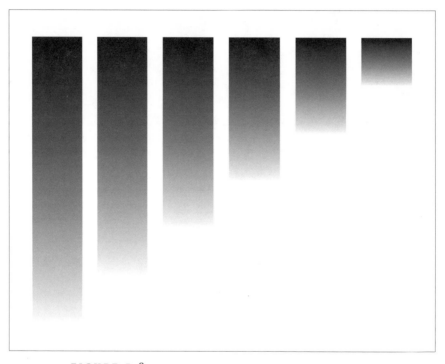

FIGURE 5.8
By changing the dot shape, the dot join effect is considerably reduced. This is the elliptical dot.

The simple round dot spot function

The simple round dot spot function of Figure 5.1

```
{dup mul exch dup mul add 1 exch sub}
```

is equivalent to

$$[1- (x^2 + y^2)] = \text{pixel order number}$$

Any given pixel's x and y coordinates fall between –1 and 1 in the halftone cell coordinate system, and for each set of x,y pixel coordinates the spot function must return a pixel order number between –1 and 1. Thus, $-1 \leq x \leq 1$ and $-1 \leq y \leq 1$, and the result of applying the spot function procedure to these two numbers must be a single pixel order number, such that $-1 \leq$ (pixel order number) ≤ 1.

The pixel order number is relative. It merely serves to establish the order in which the pixels are turned on to produce the dot. However, in cases where the pixel order numbers are compressed into a very small range (all pixel numbers within zero and 0.01), you may encounter odd behavior that makes it difficult to attain a good dot structure. Pixels with equivalent order numbers are ordered arbitrarily by the **setscreen** operator.

Looking again at the round dot spot function, squaring both the x and y coordinate numbers and adding them (via **dup mul exch dup mul add**) produces a circular ordering of the pixels, with $0 \leq$ (pixel order number) ≤ 2. Some action must now be taken to place the pixel order numbers inside the required -1 to 1 range. Depending on how you do this, you can maintain the pixel ordering or invert it. For example, subtracting $(x^2 + y^2)$ from 1, multiplying $(x^2 + y^2)$ by -0.5, and dividing $(x^2 + y^2)$ by -2 are all equivalent. They give a round dot that starts with small circles in the highlights and grows evenly throughout the tone range, forming negative dots with even four-cornered cusps in the shadows. Thus any of the following three spot functions deliver the round dot shown in Figure 5.1:

```
{dup mul exch dup mul add 1 exch sub}

{dup mul exch dup mul add -.5 mul}

{dup mul exch dup mul add -2 div}
```

On the other hand, subtracting 1 from $(x^2 + y^2)$, multiplying $(x^2 + y^2)$ by 0.5, dividing $(x^2 + y^2)$ by 2, or adding -1 to $(x^2 + y^2)$ gives an inverted round dot. Any of the following spot functions deliver the dot shown in Figure 5.4:

```
{dup mul exch dup mul add 1 sub}

{dup mul exch dup mul add 2 div}

{dup mul exch dup mul add .5 mul}

{dup mul exch dup mul add -1 add}
```

Other spot functions can achieve similar round dot results. The best dots are usually represented with simple geometric shapes that can be expressed in many different ways.

Inverting the pixel state

Most imagesetters provide a means for the operator to invert the pixel state of the output recorder as the rasterized image is exposed on film. If this is done it inverts the pixels but not the spot function, giving a true negative image. As you can see by comparing Figures 5.1 and 5.4, inversion is not an insignificant consideration.

It is often desirable to set image inversion with the application on a per-job basis rather than at the imagesetter; therefore a common practice is to use the PostScript language transfer function to invert the screen via the familiar {1 **exch sub**}. This puts the shadow dots in the highlight regions and vice-versa, which is fine if the shadow dots are inverted versions of the highlight dots, but a potential problem if they aren't.

Thus, if you are creating a film negative with a tonally asymmetrical dot—one in which the dot forms differently above and below the 50 percent gray level—transfer function inversion by itself isn't advisable. The device pixels must be inverted, but you can't be there to make sure the "invert" button gets pushed. If you use tonally asymmetrical dots, you'll need to address this issue at the implementation level. You can invert the pixel ordering via the following PostScript code:

```
currentscreen [exch /exec cvx /neg cvx] cvx
bind setscreen
```

Transfer function inversion *or* pixel inversion at the device works fine with tonally symmetrical dots. For this reason, you may wish to confine your efforts to tonally symmetrical spot functions. The Euclidean dot spot function produces such a dot, as do the diamond dot spot function in Figure 5.3 and the rhomboid dot spot function in Figure 5.6.

The Euclidean spot function

Figure 5.2 shows the current default spot function in most PostScript language implementations:

```
{abs exch abs 2 copy add 1 gt
  {1 sub dup mul exch 1 sub dup mul add 1 sub}
  {dup mul exch dup mul add 1 exch sub}
ifelse}
```

This composite dot mixes simple round dots and inverted round dots. It relies on the **abs exch abs** at the beginning of the spot function to keep the inverted-circle procedure {1 **sub dup mul**...} from exceeding the spot function limits. By varying the test value 1, you can control the transition point at which the dots invert.

The diamond dot spot function

Figure 5.3 shows the result of the diamond dot spot function. Designed for use in a variety of imaging circumstances, this composite spot function provides variables that you can use to modify the dot. Here is the spot function set up for symmetrical development across the tone range, with midtone diamonds 85 percent as wide as they are long:

```
{abs exch abs 2 copy add .75 le
  {dup mul exch dup mul add 1 exch sub}
  {2 copy add 1.25 le
    {.85 mul add 1 exch sub}
    {1 sub dup mul exch 1 sub dup mul add 1 sub}
  ifelse}ifelse}
```

The 0.75 value determines the point at which the highlight circles turn to midtone diamonds, the 1.25 value determines the point at which the midtone diamonds turn to inverted circles, and the 0.85 value determines the width of the diamond's short axis relative to its long axis. Any of these variables can be changed, so you can experiment with this dot for different tonal effects.

Inverted elliptical spot function

In Figure 5.5 the inverted round dot spot function has been modified slightly to produce an ellipse:

```
{dup mul .9 mul exch dup mul add 1 sub}
```

The 0.9 **mul** shortens one of the dot axes relative to the other. You can vary the axis width by varying this number; it's best to stay above 0.7 to avoid creating a dot that is too narrow in the highlights and shadows. Also, the smaller this factor, the longer the tonal zone over which the dots are joined at one axis only. This gives the character of a rough line screen, which can be quite visible (and sensitive to slur on press). You usually want to spread the tone jump over as small a range as possible to minimize this effect.

A noninverted elliptical dot has poor shadow behavior due to the elongated cusps in the remaining white areas.

Rhomboid dot spot function

The rhomboid dot shown in Figure 5.6 takes a simple square dot,

```
{abs exch abs add 2 div}
```

and adds a term to shorten one axis to create a rhombus (diamond) shape:

```
{abs exch abs .9 mul add 2 div}
```

Again, you can vary the width factor. As with the elliptical dot, avoid making the dots too narrow.

Spot function offsets and rosette form

As discussed in Chapter Four, the rosette produced by three superimposed screens depends on the relative positions of the screens. By moving the 45-degree screen half a dot, you can change the rosette from dot centered to clear centered, or vice versa.

This minor move is often performed on stripping tables, but preimposed film eliminates the stripping step. To fine-tune the position of the screens of PostScript code, you can use spot-function offsets for the 45-degree screen. The following example applies a half-cell offset to the halftone cell's x and y coordinates. The spot function uses the new coordinates to assign the pixel ordering in the threshold array.

A generic halftone screen call for the 45-degree screen looks like this:

```
LPI 45
{ put spot function here} bind
setscreen
```

Here's the call with code added to offset the screen:

```
LPI 45
{
  1 add 1 gt {2 sub} if exch
  1 add 1 gt {2 sub} if exch
  { put spot function here} exec
} bind
setscreen
```

You can experiment with different offset values. Keep in mind you must work within the −1 to 1 range for both original and offset cell coordinates.

Spot function offsets may affect dot formation, leading to artifacts in certain circumstances. Make sure that you examine the dots in the 45-degree screen carefully in a full white-to-black tone ramp if you use a spot function offset.

In the process of converting negative film to positive images, the rosette form inverts along with the tones. In order to have clear-centered rosettes on the press sheet, you must have dot-centered rosettes on the negative.

Using bind with spot functions

To improve performance of the **setscreen** operator it's a good idea to apply the PostScript language **bind** operator to your spot function procedures, as follows:

```
LPI angle { put spot function here} bind setscreen
```

This makes the screening calculations faster the first time the screen is called. Subsequent screening operations with the cached screen are not affected by the presence or absence of **bind** with the spot function.

Spot functions should not use operators that have side effects in the PostScript language (**def**, for example). If such operators are present the screen cannot be cached, and thus will always run slowly.

Changing the gray mapping

Three mechanisms are available for changing an image's gray mapping:

- Use an application program designed for the purpose to modify image gray (or color) content for aesthetic or production purposes.
- Modify the PostScript language transfer function to calibrate the gray-response of an imagesetter after other adjustments (such as exposure) have been made, or to produce a negative image with a tonally symmetrical dot.
- Use the PostScript Level 2 color-space transformations as designed for device color characterization, color transformations, and related color management purposes.

At times the unconventional use of these mechanisms presents an attractive way to solve a specific problem. For example, application programmers have used the transfer function for special image effects, and the halftoning mechanism is used in the Macintosh® environment for fill patterns (brick wall, fish scales, and so on). However, such uses often present complications downstream in the production process. Thus it's advisable to use each of the mechanisms for its intended purpose only.

Importance of dot shape

Dot shape becomes a key performance factor once moiré patterns are removed as a screen problem. It takes practice to write spot functions. You can use the ones presented here as is, slightly modify them as described in this chapter, or write new ones. Refer to the Bibliography for help with creating your own.

Quantization Effects in Raster-Based Halftoning

Since PostScript screening is digital halftoning, classic digital effects show up in tone, angle, and frequency. This chapter discusses these effects, which readers who have worked with PostScript screening from the beginning will recognize. The PixelBurst coprocessor addresses the tonal effects (in addition to its primary task of accelerating rendering), and Adobe Accurate Screens software addresses the angle and frequency effects.

Quantization error

Digital systems trade continuity for efficiency. The time domain offers a familiar example: compare a digital watch with a traditional one. The digital watch confidently tells you the time to the minute. The analog watch, however, tells the time within the minute—or even within the second if your eye is quick enough.

Digital systems are precise, and precision gives the impression of certainty. However, every digital system has an inherent *quantization error*. Even though it probably keeps better time over an extended period than the analog watch, a digital watch with one-minute resolution can't tell you the time to the second—in using such a watch you accept a quantization error of ±30 seconds. If a digital watch tells the time to the second, the error is smaller but still present; now it's ±0.5 seconds.

In digital halftoning, quantization errors appear in both tone and space. Tonal quantization appears in the form of contouring (shade-stepping) in blends that are supposed to represent smoothly changing tone. Spatial quantization appears as a limited selection of screens. In the commercially usable frequency range, only a small selection of angle and frequency combinations has been available in PostScript screening until recently.

Error diffusion and cell balancing

Error diffusion is a tool that reduces the effect of tonal quantization errors. Two of the dithers in Figure 2.3 provide an excellent example: compare the dispersed dot ordered dither, which shows significant tonal quantization, with the dispersed dot diffusion dither, which diffuses the quantization errors mathematically.

Applied skillfully, error diffusion gives the effect of many more tonal values than a digital system could otherwise represent. For example, in Figure 2.3 the diffusion dither manages to reproduce the effect of more tonal values than the dispersed dot ordered dither. Nothing comes for free, however; in many cases, error diffusion techniques require additional calculation and processing time.

Error diffusion can be used to good effect in clustered dot dithering also. The PixelBurst coprocessor provides error diffusion as an option to system designers. In cases where the halftone cell is not large enough to contain 255 pixels, this can effectively eliminate obvious tonal contouring.

To adjust for spatial quantization, Adobe Accurate Screens software uses *cell balancing*, a technique that distributes variations over a large area. This technique makes it possible to provide a much wider selection of screen angles and frequencies than was previously available in PostScript screening (cell balancing is not error diffusion).

Building dots with dots

Every image created on an imagesetter is built with device pixels. This holds true for halftone dots as well as line art. Thus, an imagesetter's halftone dots are built from other, smaller dots—an obvious setup for quantization errors. These errors affect four aspects of halftone screens: the number of available values (grays), the dot structure, the screen angle, and the screen frequency.

Quantization errors in halftone dots become more significant as the screen frequency increases. At higher frequencies the screens become finer, reducing the size of the halftone cell. Since the pixel size is fixed, a smaller cell reduces the number of pixels the cell can contain—and the number of tonal values it can represent at one tonal value per pixel. Imagesetter resolutions below 2000 dpi can deliver perfectly acceptable text and line art images, but tonal quantization errors often become significant with screens of usable frequency. For a small cell in color work, the quantization errors that arise in angle and frequency of the screen are even more severe than the tonal limitations.

Three approaches to screen generation

Assume you have a pixel-based system, and want this system to generate halftone screens at all angles, and at common screen frequencies between about 85 LPI and 200 LPI. In commercial digital screening you can accomplish this in one of three ways:

1. You can generate a practically unlimited selection of screens by calculating the on-off pixel state for each halftone dot on the fly and applying some limited error diffusion in the process. This requires costly hardware in the form of a fast, dedicated halftoning computer. This method has been used for years by non-PostScript screening vendors.

2. You can generate a wide selection of screens by calculating halftone dots via threshold arrays and applying some cell balancing to even out the quantization effects. This requires a clever algorithm that runs on a powerful multifunction computing machine—a powerful PostScript RIP, for example. This is the method used by Adobe Accurate Screens software.

3. You can generate a very limited selection of screens by calculating halftone dots via threshold arrays and doing nothing to even out the quantization effects. You accept quantization limits in the interests of economy and speed. This requires a less expensive multifunction computing machine—a less powerful PostScript RIP, for example. This third method is used in RT Screening, the basis for PostScript screening before Adobe Accurate Screens software. RT stands for *rational tangent.*

A discussion of RT Screening, which uses the third approach to screen generation, provides a short course in quantizations errors in pixel-based screening. Since all digital screening systems must cope with these errors one way or another, the rest of this chapter examines RT Screening in detail.

RT Screening and the halftone cell

RT Screening is based on a single square halftone cell. To minimize threshold array calculations, this one cell is used without variation for every dot in the halftone screen. Quantization effects are allowed to fall where they may.

When the user requests a halftone screen with a certain imagesetter resolution, screen angle, screen frequency (LPI), and spot function, Adobe's implementation of RT Screening:

1. Checks to see if the requested screen is available in the screen cache, and if so, skips to step 6 below and uses the cached threshold array for halftoning;

2. Establishes the ideal coordinates for the corners of the square halftone cell, using the requested frequency and angle, basic trigonometry, and the Pythagorean theorem, if the screen has not been requested previously;

3. Snaps the cell coordinates to the nearest device-pixel corner, changing the angle and frequency in the process, if the ideal cell-corner coordinates do not exactly line up with device-pixel corners (as is usually the case);

4. Refers to the PostScript language spot function to calculate the pixel ordering within the resulting cell, assigns threshold values to the pixels according to their order, and builds a threshold array based on 255 gray levels; if there are more than 255 pixels in the cell, some pixels with adjacent order numbers are assigned the same threshold value;

5. Stores the resulting screen data structures in a halftone screen cache to eliminate recalculation in case the same screen is requested in the future;

6. Uses the threshold array to compare the threshold value of each device pixel with the tonal value of the underlying image data at that location; if the image value exceeds the threshold value, the device pixel is turned on.

Obviously the above steps represent significant work for the RIP, so even this relatively simple halftoning approach is far from trivial. Depending on the implementation, the actual mechanism may operate more efficiently than the description implies, but the mathematical outcome is the same.

The halftone cell

So far the discussions of the halftone cell have left a few loose ends. These rules apply to the halftone cell in RT Screening:

- The halftone cell is square, or as nearly square as possible given its jagged outline when rotated.
- The halftone cell outline is chosen to offer the closest available match to the requested angle and frequency, accepting any quantization error.
- All four corners of the cell coincide exactly with corners of device pixels, and the jagged boundaries of the cell coincide

exactly with device-pixel boundaries. This results in a symmetrical, repeatable halftone cell.

- Angles that coincide with the geometry of the pixel grid are delivered exactly. These are usually 0, 90, and 45 degrees.
- The cell—with its jagged outline—must "tile" seamlessly with its neighbors on all four sides. Every device pixel must belong to one and only one halftone cell. (The actual tiling used by the RIP may differ from the tiling defined by the cell edges. This has no effect on this concept or the math.)
- The cell affords $(n^2 + 1)$ gray levels, where n is the length in pixels on the side of the square cell. There is one gray level for each pixel in the cell, plus an additional one for the case in which all pixels are off. (For this formula to work with rotated cells, you usually must use fractional pixel lengths for the cell side.)
- There is no specific requirement for the cell's pixel count, but there is a ceiling on the number of pixels allowed in the cell. This usually takes the form of a lower implementation limit on frequency. Many high-resolution implementations place this limit at approximately 10 LPI.

The RIP must follow these rules for any size cell. The smaller the cell, the fewer the pixels it contains, and the larger the quantization errors. For any device resolution the screen choices are more numerous for large cells (lower frequency), but dwindle as cell size becomes relatively small (higher frequency). With RT Screening one way to reduce quantization errors is to increase the resolution.

A small halftone cell at 0 degrees

A small cell oriented at 0 degrees relative to the device grid offers the simplest example of the choices that must be made by the RIP. Figure 6.1 shows a 5-pixel-square cell oriented at exactly 0 degrees. On a 300 dpi device such a cell represents a 60 LPI screen; on a 2400 dpi device it represents a 480 LPI screen. Quantization errors are severe for every parameter:

- The small cell resolves grays poorly, affording only 26 gray levels; they are almost 4 percent apart, which is highly visible in circumstances where grays are changing, such as in gray blends and tone ramps. (In areas where there is no gray change, even this severe quantization often goes unnoticed.)

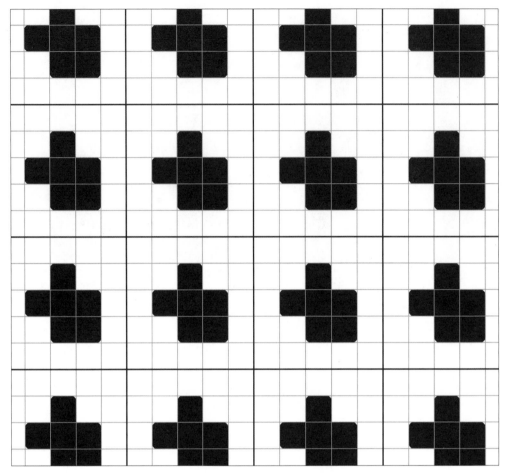

FIGURE 6.1

A 24 percent dot in a 0-degree screen based on an invariant cell of 25 pixels. The cell boundaries are indicated by the black lines.

- The frequency is highly quantized; the RIP delivers this same cell in circumstances where the number of pixels on a cell side is between 4.5 and 5.5. Thus, a 300 dpi device delivers this 60.00 LPI cell for any request between 54.54 LPI and 66.66 LPI. At 0 degrees the next higher choice is a 4-by-4 cell of 75 LPI; the next lower choice is a 6-by-6 cell of 50 LPI. Similarly, a 2400 dpi device delivers this 480.00 LPI cell for any request between 436.37 LPI and 533.33 LPI. The next higher choice is a 4-by-4 cell of 600 LPI; the next lower choice is a 6-by-6 cell of 400 LPI.
- Finally, the angle is quantized—an important issue covered in detail later. With this small cell the next higher available angle

at approximately the same LPI is 11.3099 degrees; the next
lower available angle is −11.3099 degrees.

A small halftone cell at 45 degrees

An angle of 0 degrees lines up with the device pixels, so a request for a
0-degree screen angle is easy to fulfill. Another easy-to-fulfill angle is
45 degrees. A small cell oriented at 45 degrees illustrates some of the compromises that occur as the cell is rotated. In Figure 6.2 the screen is angled at
45 degrees relative to the device-pixel grid. The nominal cell boundary is
indicated by the solid black square coincident with the cell corners.

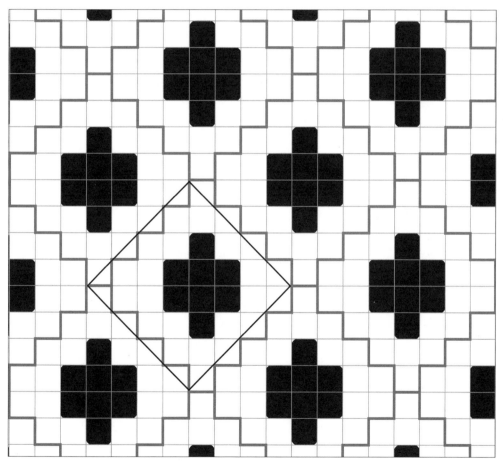

FIGURE 6.2

*A 45 percent screen based on an invariant cell of 32 pixels. The nominal cell
boundary is indicated by the black line.*

Since the cell boundary is angled 4 pixels over and 4 pixels up, by the Pythagorean theorem the cell side is 5.657 pixels:

$$\sqrt{4^2 + 4^2} = 5.657$$

A cell side of 5.657 pixels is 53.033 LPI on a 300 dpi device. The next lower cell side at 45 degrees is 4.243 pixels:

$$\sqrt{3^2 + 3^2} = 4.243$$

which is 70.71 LPI on a 300 dpi device.

Thus, the angle and the frequency interact. Suppose you request a 60 LPI screen at various angles on a 300 dpi device. Requesting 0 degrees gets you a 60 LPI, 0-degree screen. A 60 LPI request at 45 degrees, on the other hand, produces a 53.033 LPI screen at 45 degrees. (This is the actual default screen on many 300 dpi laser printers—even though the default screen *request* on such devices is often 60 LPI at 45 degrees.)

Requests for screen angles other than 0 and 45 degrees are seldom met exactly. In such cases both angle and frequency are subject to quantization error.

A larger cell at 30 degrees

Figure 6.3 shows a hypothetical cell resulting from a request for a 133 LPI, 15-degree screen on a 2400 dpi device using RT Screening. The nearest appropriate device-pixel corner is 17 pixels over and 5 pixels up, so the actual screen is 135.44 LPI at 16.3895 degrees. The distance between cell corners is 17.72 pixels, so the cell has 314 pixels (17.72 squared is 314).

With this cell the quantization effects are much smaller than those encountered with the 5-by-5 cell. Tone reproduction is no problem; with 314 pixels to work with, the cell can assign all 256 threshold values available in the PostScript language. (Since every one of the 314 pixels must have a threshold value, 58 pixels will share identical values.)

The angle and frequency, however, still show significant variations from the request. The angle is off by 1.3895 degrees and the frequency is off by 2.44 LPI. To avoid shifts in the rosette form in color printing in the 100 to 200 LPI range, angle inaccuracies of no more than 0.001 degrees and frequency inaccuracies of no more than 0.01 LPI should be considered the minimum acceptable variations *when you are using the traditional screening model based on 15 degrees, 75 degrees, and equal screen frequencies.* Adobe Accurate Screens software provides many screens within these tolerances. New methods of superimposing screens offer better performance and also build traditional rosettes, as discussed in later chapters.

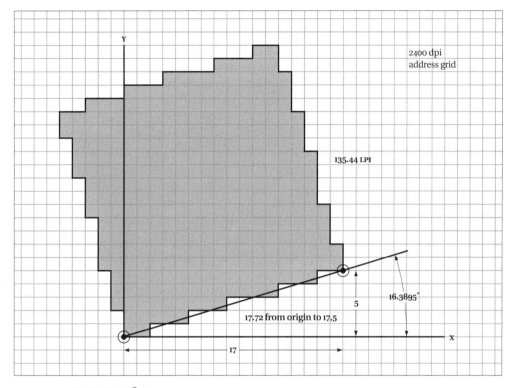

FIGURE 6.3

A nominal 133.33 LPI (18x18) cell rotated a nominal 15 degrees on a 2400 dpi device. The cell has contracted to give a higher frequency, and the angle is inaccurate.

The math of the rational tangent

In the drive to duplicate traditional process-color screen assignments on digital systems, approximating the irrational tangent angles of 15 and 75 degrees has been the goal of many digital inventors. Ironically, now that these angles can be achieved for practical purposes, it turns out they are no longer indispensable for high-quality color printing. Nonetheless, a review of rational tangents may make it easier for you to understand process-color screening. It will also pave the way for the discussion of supercell theory in Chapter Seven.

In RT Screening, every halftone cell is identical. The angle and frequency options for the entire screen are constrained; *they are those of the single cell.* To illustrate the limitations this imposes, in Figure 6.4 a model of a halftone cell at 0 degrees is placed so its lower-left corner is at the origin of the Cartesian coordinate system and its lower-right corner is on the x axis a certain (integral) number of pixels to the right (Figure 6.4a). This cell is then rotated counterclockwise by a requested angle (Figure 6.4b). For any requested rotation except 45 degrees, there's a good chance that the lower-right corner of the cell no longer coincides exactly with a pixel corner. However, the cell corner *must* coincide with a pixel corner. The cell adjusts, snapping to the nearest pixel corner as in Figure 6.4c. It incurs some quantization error in the process—the cell side stretches and the angle changes.

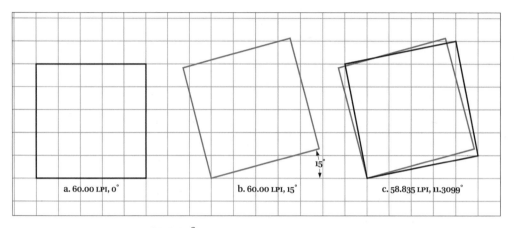

a. 60.00 LPI, 0°   b. 60.00 LPI, 15°   15°   c. 58.835 LPI, 11.3099°

FIGURE 6.4

Quantization error in RT Screening on a 300 dpi device. The black outlines indicate actual halftone cells; the gray outlines indicate hypothetical cells.

"Snapping to the nearest pixel corner" is a convenient way of saying that the x and y coordinates of the cell's lower-right corner are rounded off to integers. As a result of this operation the cell rotation in Figure 6.4c is now an angle whose tangent is two integers—the first integer is the number of pixels up and the second integer is the number of pixels over, measured from the lower-left corner to the lower-right corner of the cell. Thus, the cell in Figure 6.4 is rotated not by the requested 15 degrees (which meets no pixel corner exactly), but by 11.3099 degrees, which has a tangent of exactly 1/5 (one up, five over). This tangent is a ratio of integers—a *rational tangent*. (It may help to think RATIOnal tangent.)

How close is good enough?

Ancient mathematicians argued that any number could be represented as the fraction (ratio) of two integers if these integers could be arbitrarily large. It was eventually proven that this is not so; in fact, *most* real numbers cannot be expressed as the ratio of integers. These are the *irrational* numbers. Among the many examples are the square root of two, the tangent of 15 degrees, and pi.

The reason for the ancient confusion is that it's possible, using simple integer ratios, to get *close* to any real number via a process of successive approximation using fractions with ever-larger denominators. The ancients assumed that this could go on for only so long—the fraction's denominator would become large enough to allow you to nail a given number directly on the nose if you used the proper numerator. In reality, though, successive approximation can (and usually does) go on forever. You get very, very close to any number as the integers in the ratio become astronomically large, but you can seldom express an arbitrary number *exactly* by a ratio of integers.

In real life, however, really close is usually good enough. Increasing accuracy by using larger integers in the tangent ratios is a key concept behind Adobe Accurate Screens software and the supercell discussed in the next chapter. If your aim is to approximate a given screen, Adobe Accurate Screens software can do it. However, if your aim is to use any digital system to *exactly* generate a requested screen whose angle has an irrational tangent, you are out of luck. No digital method can accomplish this mathematically, because digital device pixels correspond to integers.

If you are using the traditional color screening model based on 15- and 75- degree angles, how close a screen angle is close enough? In color screening, as noted earlier, angular accuracy of about 0.001 degrees and frequency accuracy of about 0.01 LPI is a minimum. For images of approximately 8 by 10 inches and up, variation within 0.0004 degrees and 0.002 LPI has been shown to produce excellent results. Beyond this level the imprecision of the physical world begins to intrude and further accuracy becomes "lost in the noise."

However, accuracy is not dependent on approximation of irrational tangent angles. As discussed in Chapter Nine, screens can be combined in such a way that minor deviations from 15 and 75 degrees are compensated for by a complementary deviation in the LPI of the 45-degree screen.

Breaking free of the one-cell restriction

RT Screening keeps the integers in the tangent ratio small in the interest of speed and economy, and since the ratio is tied tightly to dimensions of the halftone cell, the cell is small. If the cell grows due to lower frequency, higher resolution, or both, it contains more pixels. As a result, the integers in the ratio can increase. This provides more possibilities for cell rotation, which in turn increases the number of potential screens.

If you could break free of the mathematical constraints imposed by RT Screening's halftone-cell model, you could generate many more screens— and have a much better chance of finding good screen combinations for color screen sets. Since bigger cells give more screening possibilities, why not use *giant* cells, each of which contains many smaller halftone cells? These giant cells are *supercells*, the subject of Chapter Seven.

Is it an error?

Finally, a semantic—but far from incidental—discussion is appropriate. Ignoring the engineering conventions for a moment, does a limited set of angles and frequencies really cause error? You can look at it two ways. If you request one angle and frequency combination but the computer gives you a different one, you might consider the difference between your request and the actual screen an error. But, if all the available angle and frequency combinations are known well in advance, might not the true error lie in your *request*? For example, if you know you can obtain 133.333 LPI at 0 degrees but insist on requesting 133.000 LPI at 0 degrees, perhaps your request has an error of 0.333 LPI.

In color printing, traditional screen assignments owe nothing to digital technology. In turn, digital screening technology need not be bound by tradition. You can achieve the desired outcome—a consistent rosette—with nontraditional digital screen assignments.

Given the narrow tolerances for variation in superimposed screens, it's very difficult to build good rosettes with a limited selection of screens, even if you use nontraditional screen assignments. A logical solution to this problem is to provide a wider selection of screen angles and frequencies. Adobe Accurate Screens software accomplishes this, providing thousands of screens whereas RT Screening provides only a few dozen.

The task of the screen developer is to combine screens well. Blind adherence to traditional screening prescriptions can lead a developer to miss many excellent digital opportunities. The real development goal is to find ideal combinations that build excellent rosettes—using traditional and nontraditional angle and frequency assignments as needed.

Supercell Concepts

As shown in Chapter Six, the digital nature of the imagesetter pixel grid imposes severe constraints on the number of available halftone screens when these screens are based on a small halftone cell. Clearly a more versatile approach is needed to obtain a wider, more usable selection of screens at a reasonable cost. For Adobe Accurate Screens software, this more versatile approach uses the supercell. This chapter discusses supercells in general.

If you use PostScript software to produce high-quality color printed materials, this is the real-world color-screening challenge for your RIP:

- Within each of the commonly used frequency ranges, the RIP should deliver a set of four halftone screens that, when super-imposed, produce the moiré-free images necessary for current high-quality color printing.
- The imaging process should not take an inordinate amount of time once you press the print button.
- The RIP should be of reasonable cost and complexity.

In other words, the challenge is for high-quality, fast turnaround, and moderate cost. As in most real-world situations, these goals conflict. Fortunately, in PostScript screening the RIPs are getting better, faster, and relatively less expensive. With Adobe Accurate Screens software halftoning, the super-cell gets a substantial portion of the credit.

Cell size and screen choices

With RT Screening, a request for a 133.33 LPI, 15-degree screen on a 2400 dpi imagesetter produces a screen of 135.44 LPI and 16.39 degrees (Figure 6.3). This is due to the small cell size. The closest cell you can build to fulfill the request has its lower-right corner 17 pixels over and 5 pixels up from its lower-left corner. The selection of screens is severely limited. Table 7.1 shows the six screens closest to the request. Notice how far apart these neighboring screens are in angle, frequency, or both.

TABLE 7.1

Screens closest to requested 133.33 LPI, 15-degree screen on a 2400 dpi device.

Lower-right corner	Angle	Frequency
16 pixels over, 4 pixels up:	14.03°	145.52 LPI
16 pixels over, 5 pixels up:	17.35°	143.17 LPI
17 pixels over, 4 pixels up:	13.24°	137.42 LPI
17 pixels over, 5 pixels up:	16.39°	135.44 LPI
17 pixels over, 6 pixels up:	19.44°	133.13 LPI
18 pixels over, 5 pixels up:	15.52°	128.47 LPI

The supercell offers an answer to this problem. Like its smaller halftone cell cousins in RT Screening, a supercell is square. Like the RT Screening halftone cells, supercell corners must align exactly with pixel corners, and the supercell must tile seamlessly with itself. Unlike the RT Screening cells, however, a typical supercell contains many halftone cells. Within the supercell these halftone cells need not be uniform and need not be square, which opens the door to a much wider selection of screens.

The neighboring screens produced with Adobe Accurate Screens software typically lie within 0.01 degrees and 0.05 LPI of one another, and often closer. As the amount of memory available for screening calculations increases, the number of available screens increases, the gaps between screens become smaller, and the threshold array becomes more complex. The time required for the threshold array calculations increases also, although this calculation is required only once—then the screen is cached.

Bigger is better—if you're flexible

Given the digital nature of the device pixel grid and the mathematical reality of rational tangents, a large cell outline offers more screen possibilities than a small one. To illustrate this concept, the halftone cell shown in Figure 6.3—which resulted from a request for 133.33 LPI at 15 degrees—forms the starting point for Figure 7.1. If you expand this cell's boundaries roughly threefold in each direction, you get a bigger cell outline, and an improved choice of cell-corner placements. In Figure 7.1, by placing the lower-right corner 52 pixels over and 14 pixels up, the angle of the large cell becomes 15.0685 degrees, significantly closer to the original request of 15 degrees.

On a 2400 dpi device this large cell gives a screen frequency of about 45 LPI. But suppose you could subdivide this large cell into nine halftone cells! If the division were ideal, the resulting halftone screen would be 133.701 LPI at 15.0685 degrees. The large cell would let you come much closer to the original screen request.

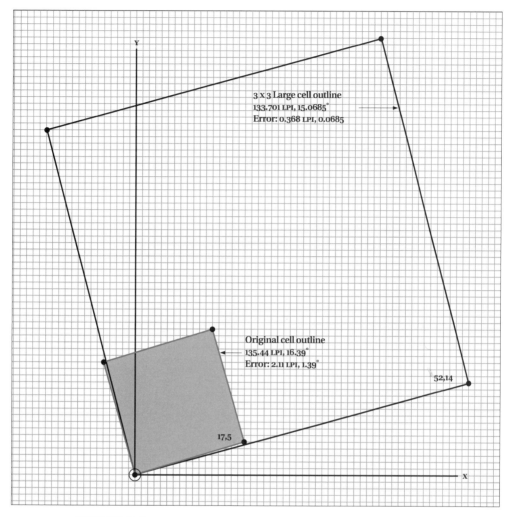

Original cell outline
135.44 LPI, 16.39°
Error: 2.11 LPI, 1.39°

3 x 3 Large cell outline
133.701 LPI, 15.0685°
Error: 0.368 LPI, 0.0685

52,14

17,5

FIGURE 7.1

Outlines of a small halftone cell and a large 3x3 cell. Both attempt to deliver a 133.33 LPI, 15-degree screen. This large cell is much more accurate than the smaller cell.

It won't suffice to subdivide the large cell into nine *identical* halftone cells, however. A large cell consisting of nine halftone-cell clones is just as inaccurate as any one of the clones (Figure 7.2). If you take a single halftone cell with cell corners that line up exactly with pixel corners, and then simply clone this cell nine times, the corners of all the clones fall exactly on pixel corners, too. These cloned cells would force the large cell to have the very same angle and frequency as each of the clones—it's RT Screening all over again.

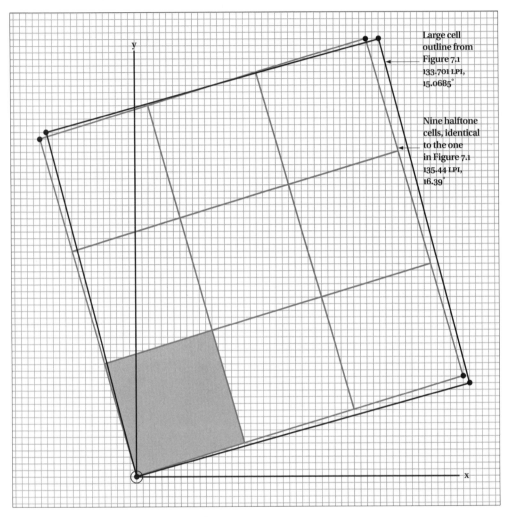

Large cell
outline from
Figure 7.1
133.701 LPI,
15.0685°

Nine halftone
cells, identical
to the one
in Figure 7.1
135.44 LPI,
16.39°

FIGURE 7.2
*Compare the outline of nine identical halftone cells with the large cell outline.
The large cell gives a better approximation of the desired 133.33 LPI, 15-degree
screen.*

You can take another approach, however. You can position the large cell
outline for greatest accuracy and then divide it evenly into nine average cells.
The corners of these average cells don't fall exactly on pixel corners (Figure
7.3). These average cells can't be halftone cells—you can't split pixels. But if
you can figure a way to fit nine average cells into the large cell outline, you will
have a more accurate screen.

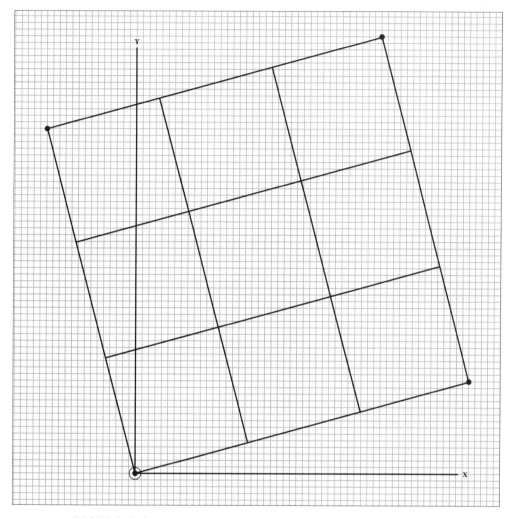

FIGURE 7.3

When the large cell outline of Figure 7.1 is evenly divided into nine halftone cells, the cell corners don't match up with pixel corners, with the exception of the large cell's corners.

The solution is to build nine separate halftone cells, each of which has corners that land on a pixel corner address, and each of which is as close as possible in size and shape to the average cell. To accomplish this, the nine halftone cells *must vary slightly* within the large cell.

Turning a large cell into a supercell

The previous example illustrates a key concept: To achieve greater accuracy a large cell can't simply be a scaled-up replica of a small halftone cell. For a large cell outline to be useful as a supercell, you must vary the individual half-tone cells within it, in both shape and number of pixels contained.

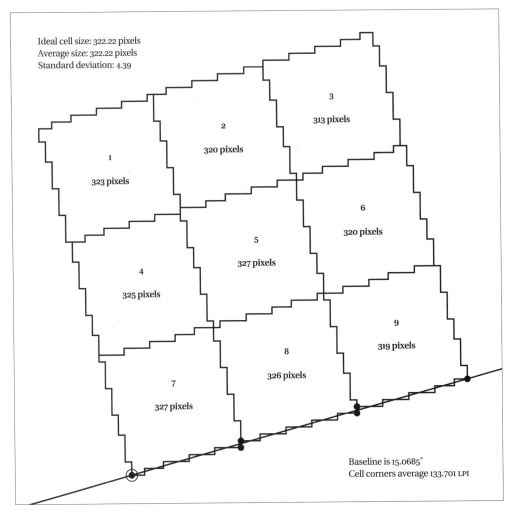

Ideal cell size: 322.22 pixels
Average size: 322.22 pixels
Standard deviation: 4.39

3
313 pixels

2
320 pixels

1
323 pixels

6
320 pixels

5
327 pixels

4
325 pixels

9
319 pixels

8
326 pixels

7
327 pixels

Baseline is 15.0685°
Cell corners average 133.701 LPI

FIGURE 7.4

The first attempt at building a supercell of nine 18x18 halftone cells results, as expected, in a variety of cell sizes and outlines. Cell balancing reduces the actual cell variation. Even so, supercell halftone dots vary from one cell to the next at the same gray level.

So, to approximate a given requested screen frequency and screen angle, you first assign the supercell corners for maximum accuracy. In doing this you define the supercell outline (since the supercell is square). You then fill the supercell outline with individual halftone cells, adjusting them slightly to fit. For any given halftone cell this involves a change in both size and shape, but the *average* cell size remains the same (Figure 7.4). Note that the supercell in Figure 7.4 is illustrative only. With supercells produced by Adobe Accurate Screens technology, the individual halftone cells vary more in form and vary less in size, usually within a pixel or two of one another.

The fundamental difference between RT Screening and supercell screening is this: in RT Screening every halftone cell is identical, whereas in supercell screening, the halftone cells are permitted—required—to vary. The variation is distributed as evenly as possible over the entire supercell.

Supercell size

A supercell can expand as necessary to better approximate a requested screen angle and screen frequency. In cases where a single halftone cell can perfectly represent the requested screen frequency and screen angle, no improvement is gained by using a supercell.

In other cases, requested screens are approximated better as the supercell grows larger. Supercell sizes range from a few halftone cells to 3000 halftone cells or more. Supercell size limitations are imposed by the RAM available for screen calculation (screen space), and the processing speed (the time a user is willing to devote to first-time screen calculations before caching). Once calculated and cached, however, screens based on large supercells offer no penalty in imaging speed.

Tiling

The supercell represents the first stage of screen calculation. The actual threshold array takes the form of a tile. Tiles can take many shapes; a simple tiling scheme is shown in Figure 7.5. For any given screen the time and computational effort required to calculate the initial tile may be significant, but once calculated the tile is cached and used repeatedly for fast halftoning. In general, a larger tile offers faster processing.

When the interior of the tile becomes complex—as happens with supercells—the tiling calculations become more involved. As a result tiling strategies, tiling methods, and tile calculations are proprietary in nature. The discussions in this chapter are conceptual, not literal. They are designed to give you a framework for understanding and working with the Adobe Accurate Screens supercell-based screening system.

Supertiles

A supercell-based threshold array is known as a *supertile*. Although the terms supercell and supertile are sometimes used interchangeably, a tile and a cell are usually different in structure (Figure 7.5). Halftone cells and supercells are theoretical and mathematical concepts used in the calculation of the (usually large) threshold array that constitutes a supertile.

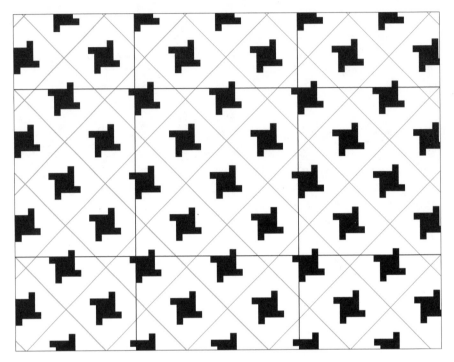

FIGURE 7.5

Tiling allows faster processing. Tile boundaries (solid lines) freely cross ideal cell boundaries (dashed lines), "splitting" dots. Each dot is made whole again by the neighboring tile. Tiles are often much larger than shown here.

Screen developers should note that the screen grid, the device pixel grid, the supercell, and the supertile all coincide reliably at one spot: the origin of the device pixel system. Check the technical information for your particular device to establish where the origin of the pixel grid lies.

Screen space

In general, the more memory available for threshold array calculations, the greater the accuracy of the screen. The amount of RAM set aside for screening calculations in Adobe Accurate Screens software is termed *screen space*. Larger amounts of screen space increase the calculation time for the building of the threshold array prior to placing it in the screen cache. Thus, screen space should be limited to the minimum necessary for the screening application. Many excellent screen sets can be obtained using minimum amounts of screen space.

Dot variation

As a result of normal halftone cell variation, imagesetter film output may surprise you the first time you check it under a loupe: the halftone dots aren't consistent in shape, even at the same level of gray. Some of the dots may look ragged. This is due to the allowable variation in the shape and size of the halftone cells. When you examine film at a magnification that makes individual pixels clear, the halftone cell variations can jump out at you (Figure 7.6). Such dot variation is typical of supercell-based screening.

© Peter Fink 1991

FIGURE 7.6
As shown in this photomicrograph, halftone cell variation is typical of supercell-based screening (a microscope pointer is visible in the upper center).

The varied halftone dots may appear unacceptable to traditional printers, who value consistent dot form. As a practical matter, however, slight halftone dot variation seems to *improve*, not degrade, the final printed image, producing smoother tone. This smoothness arises in part from the variations in halftone cell form, and in part from favorable interactions with the inherent dot-size variations produced by any given printing process.

In the printing process the individual pixels of high-resolution images are not reproduced. Individual pixel-size features on imagesetter film do not transfer reliably to printed sheets in cases where film is imageset at a resolution of 2000 dpi or above.

Screen sets

All digital halftoning is subject to quantization error. Adobe Accurate Screens software reduces this error and averages it throughout the supercell. Small though it may be, some error usually remains, and this error varies from screen to screen. Thus certain sets of screens superimpose more successfully than others and perform better in color printing. Much development activity centers around finding, testing, and improving good screen sets. Screen sets are discussed in detail in Chapters Nine through Eleven.

PART THREE

Development

Adobe Accurate Screens Software

This chapter takes a look at Adobe Accurate Screens software, discussing the implications of extensible software-based screening. It also discusses items of special interest to programmers, so some sections assume you are familiar with PostScript language dictionaries and PostScript language halftone operators and practices for both PostScript Level 1 and PostScript Level 2. You can skip over these technical areas if you want. On the other hand, if you aren't familiar with these topics and plan to write PostScript code, refer to the *PostScript Language Reference Manual*, Second Edition.

Adobe Accurate Screens software is part of the PostScript Level 2 language and is also available as an extension to the PostScript Level 1 language. For compatibility with applications that invoke Level 1 Adobe Accurate Screens halftoning, the Level 2 language supports two key Level 1 Adobe Accurate Screens operators.

Is Adobe Accurate Screens quality necessary?

As noted in earlier chapters, constructing a supercell-based threshold array requires a powerful RIP, a significant amount of RAM, and a certain amount of time for the initial computation. Since most production environments operate at a preestablished level of quality, management must decide whether the target quality-level justifies the related halftoning costs.

Many print production situations don't rely on rosettes, and therefore don't require precise matching of superimposed screens. Typical examples of rosette-free situations are one-color printing, flat tint builds in two colors, and four-color printing of artwork that requires two screens or less in any one location (other colors may be used at 100 percent coverage). In these cases it isn't necessary to use supercell-based screening.

On the other hand, once a screen's threshold array is in the screen cache, there is no time required to build the screen when it's called again. Also, as specialized rendering hardware like the PixelBurst coprocessor comes into general use, the time required for imaging will fall dramatically. In many cases, these factors make it practical to use supercell-based screens for all imagesetting, simplifying the production process.

Benefits of software-based screening

Given the calculations necessary to deliver screen angles that closely approximate irrational tangent angles, most digital halftoning systems have been hardware-based. Hardware-based systems rely on specialized screening hardware in the form of dedicated screening computers or electro-mechanical assemblies. In contrast, Adobe Accurate Screens software does not rely on hardware, although imagesetting proceeds faster with an accelerator. Typically, accelerators consist of add-on circuit boards or ASICS built into the RIP.

Aside from the equipment, the distinction between dedicated screening systems and Adobe Accurate Screens software may appear subtle until you take into account that a typical hardware-based screening system's screening methods, and often its selection of screens, are hard-wired into the physical unit. In contrast, a software-based system calculates and delivers every requested screen.

How closely the delivered screen matches the request—and how well the delivered screen superimposes with other screens for color work—is up to the screen set developer to determine. With a software-based screening system, screens and screen sets can be readily tested, easily modified, and inexpensively distributed. In the case of Adobe Accurate Screens software, an end user only needs to enter the frequency, angle, and spot function arguments to have immediate access to a new screen or screen set. With this ready testing and use, an open software-based screening system like Adobe Accurate Screens software encourages screen development. It also provides an open market for improved screens and screen sets.

Many screen developers may seek to develop color screen sets based on the conventional rosette. Much is known about this particular screening approach, so it makes sense to use it. However, Adobe Accurate Screens software places no limitation on how you superimpose its many possible screens. For example, Adobe Accurate Screens software approximates irrational tangent angles. In other cases, you can achieve the conventional rosette with excellent results by using screens that deviate slightly from irrational tangent angles (as discussed in Chapter Nine).

Adobe Accurate Screens software assumes clustered dot dithering, uses a square halftone cell, and places the halftone dots on a square grid, to the extent possible given the distortions within a supertile. These restrictions still leave ample room for innovation on the part of a screen developer.

Since many production methods call for combining screened images *after* they are output, you are often free to image any set of screens you want and combine them later. If you want to experiment with different combinations of screen angles, screen frequencies, or dot shapes, Adobe Accurate Screens software provides a convenient, flexible platform for such work. In principle, you could develop a completely new screening approach of your own, using Adobe Accurate Screens software to test your screens.

Screen set libraries

Some users of color screens require only a handful of screen sets. Others with more challenging needs welcome a wider selection. For any given output device and resolution you can build a library of screen sets, some for general use and others designed specifically for different printing situations, images, and media. As optimized screen sets become available, more users will become aware of the improved appearance they offer.

During the next several years the technology of printing will undergo dramatic changes. Some of these changes, such as the move from imagesetting on film to imaging direct to press, will affect image quality in ways that will require new screen sets for optimum performance. Widely available software-based screening encourages timely development and distribution of new libraries of screen sets as the need for them arises.

Using Adobe Accurate Screens software

From a functional, PostScript language perspective, using Adobe Accurate Screens software is straightforward. In the PostScript Level 1 extension, you set **accuratescreens** to **true**, adjust the screen space if necessary using **screenspace**, and then call **setscreen** with the standard frequency, angle, and spot function. In the PostScript Level 2 version, you can also call **sethalftone** with a well-formed halftone dictionary as the argument. This halftone dictionary must contain at least five entries: **HalftoneType** (an integer set at 1), **Frequency**, **Angle**, **SpotFunction**, and **AccurateScreens** (a boolean set to **true**). The frequency, angle, and spot function in the dictionary are the same as used in the PostScript Level 1 **setscreen** operator.

Details about the operators, parameters, and dictionaries discussed in the following sections may be found in the *PostScript Language Reference Manual* and in the supplementary documentation for your PostScript language device.

Adobe Accurate Screens PostScript Level 1 operators

Adobe Accurate Screens software on PostScript Level 1 devices uses five PostScript language operators. For the sake of compatibility, **setaccuratescreens**, **accuratescreens**, and **checkscreen** are also included in PostScript Level 2.

A brief description of the five PostScript Level 1 Adobe Accurate Screens software operators follows. Since each operator is used in the context of the operand stack, stack operands and results are provided also. The format used is the same as that used in the "Operators" chapter of the *PostScript Language Reference Manual.*

operand **operator** result
To the left of the operator is the operand (or operands), if any, that must be on the stack when the operator is called. To the right of the operator is the result (or results), if any, left on the stack by the execution of the operator. A dash indicates cases where no operand is needed or no result is placed on the stack.

The five Level 1 operators **setaccuratescreens**, **accuratescreens**, **setscreenspace**, **screenspace**, and **checkscreen** are located in **statusdict**.

bool **setaccuratescreens** —
This operator enables and disables Adobe Accurate Screens software. It is enabled if the boolean argument is *true*, and disabled if the boolean argument is *false.* The operator returns no result on the stack. This operator is supported in PostScript Level 2.

— **accuratescreens** bool
This operator queries the RIP for the current state of Adobe Accurate Screens software, and places the answer on the stack in the form of a boolean result. A boolean *true* result indicates that Adobe Accurate Screens software is enabled; a boolean *false* result indicates it is disabled. This operator is supported in PostScript Level 2.

real **setscreenspace** —
This operator establishes the amount of RAM dedicated to constructing the supertile. The maximum amount of screen space may vary with the implementation; the typical default value is 7. One unit of screen space is equivalent to approximately 100K of RAM.

— **screenspace** real
This operator queries the RIP for the current screen space and returns the result in the form of a real number.

freq angle **checkscreen** freq angle length
This operator makes it possible for the RIP to tell you the exact frequency and angle of a screen without actually building a super-

tile. You give your frequency and angle requests as real-number arguments. The operator returns the actual frequency and actual angle of the supercell that would have been used had you called **setscreen** with Adobe Accurate Screens software enabled and with the current screen space and resolution. The third result is the length, in inches, of the theoretical moiré period between the requested and actual screens; this indicates how closely the actual screen matches your request. The longer this length, the closer the match. The current halftone screen of the device is not affected by this operator, which is designed to be used with PostScript Level 1 screen set search tools.

If you plan to call these operators in your own programs, your PostScript code should query the RIP for the PostScript language level and the presence of the **checkscreen** operator.

Adobe Accurate Screens in PostScript Level 2

Imagesetters are one-color devices. So are the individual stages of multistage presses. PostScript Level 1 imagesetting devices use the familiar one-color **setscreen** operator for each screen in turn as color-separated images are output in the course of any given color production job. Once these devices incorporate PostScript Level 2, you will still be able to use **setscreen**, but you may prefer the more versatile PostScript Level 2 operator **sethalftone**.

Adobe Accurate Screens software is enabled in additional ways in PostScript Level 2. Given the numerous potential halftoning situations the PostScript language must now accommodate, PostScript Level 2 uses *halftone dictionaries* to define the current halftone screen as part of the graphics state. In PostScript Level 2, Adobe Accurate Screens software is enabled by a dictionary entry.

> halftonedict **sethalftone** —
> The **sethalftone** operator takes a halftone dictionary as its argument. It makes this the current halftone dictionary, establishing the halftone parameters within the dictionary as those of the graphics state.

For Adobe Accurate Screens halftoning you must use a halftone dictionary that contains the keys and corresponding values shown in Table 8.1:

TABLE 8.1

Key-value pairs for dictionary of HalftoneType 1.

Key	Type	Value
HalftoneType	integer	(*Required*) Must be 1. A dictionary of this type uses either RT Screening or Adobe Accurate Screens software.
Frequency	real	(*Required*) Your requested frequency.
Angle	real	(*Required*) Your requested angle.
SpotFunction	procedure	(*Required*) Your spot function.
AccurateScreens	boolean	(*Required*) To enable Adobe Accurate Screens software, this boolean must be *true*; if this boolean is *false*, or the key is omitted, RT Screening is used.
ActualFrequency	real	(*Optional*) Replaced by **sethalftone** with the actual screen frequency.
ActualAngle	real	(*Optional*) Replaced by **sethalftone** with the actual screen angle.
TransferFunction	procedure	(*Optional*) Must be a valid transfer function procedure.

The transfer function is one possible place to provide corrections for anticipated dot gain in printing. However, to avoid disturbing critical image-setter calibration—which also uses the transfer function—always concatenate dot-gain corrections with the existing transfer function.

PostScript Level 2 does not use the **screenspace** operator. Instead, screen space is reserved via the **MaxScreenStorage** and **Max ScreenItem** parameters. Refer to the *PostScript Language Reference Manual* and supplementary documentation for details.

Screen Sets

In process-color printing you superimpose four halftone screens, one for each of the colors cyan, magenta, black, and yellow. These four screens constitute a screen set. The matched screens in a good screen set superimpose without unwanted patterns. Each screen set incorporates a halftone dot shape that reproduces tone appropriately for the type of image you intend to print. A good screen set can be hard to find, but once you find it you'll rely on it.

These final three chapters focus on screen set development. This chapter discusses screen sets and various factors that affect their quality. Chapters Ten and Eleven outline a methodology for screen set development. Even if you don't plan to develop screen sets yourself, this information will help you understand what's involved.

Summary of the development process

Screen set fundamentals and screen set development are closely intertwined. The following summary of the development process serves the purposes of this chapter and establishes a context for the following chapters.

Screen set development involves five stages. These are:

- Setting quality criteria
- Choosing or developing a screen combination theory
- Searching for candidate screen sets
- Testing the candidate screen sets in a laboratory
- Testing them in the field

Adobe Accurate Screens software offers many thousands of screens. The numerous available screens and various screen-combination theories add complexity to the early stages of the development process. An efficient means of identifying and testing screen sets is crucial.

A brief example illustrates the situation. Within the narrow range from 132 LPI to 133 LPI on a 2400 dpi imagesetter at the default screen space of 7, nine screens are available at 45 degrees, 23 screens are available within 0.03 of a degree of 15 degrees, and 23 screens are also available within 0.03 of a degree of 75 degrees. If you are a screen set developer and elect to use the mirror-image pairs of 15- and 75-degree screens in combination with a 45-degree screen, this gives you a theoretical total of 207 three-screen screen sets to consider.

How many of these potential combinations yield essentially moiré-free screen sets? Perhaps three of them, according to one theory of screen combination. None of them, according to another theory. However both theories have identified different screen sets that proved excellent.

Search tools

Given the large number of screens, an automated screen set search process is called for, and PostScript language search tools are available (see Appendix A). These tools are PostScript language programs that you can open with a word processor or the LaserTalk™ application. You type your criteria for angle, frequency, and quality into the search tool and download it to a PostScript RIP (with some tools this RIP must support Adobe Accurate Screens software). As the search tool's program executes in the RIP, it considers numerous possible combinations of available screens, evaluates their potential according to the theory incorporated in the specific search tool, and delivers a report from which you select screen set candidates for testing.

Implicit in every search tool is a theory of screen combination. Various theories tend to conflict. Since any search tool is only as useful as the theory and quality criteria it incorporates, it makes sense to search the desired screen-frequency ranges with more than one tool and more than one set of quality criteria, and to test as many candidate screen sets as possible.

Testing is necessary

Once identified, candidate screen sets are tested on film to confirm the moiré forecasts of the search tools. There maybe some variation between the films and the forecasts. Many candidate sets are winnowed out at this stage. The surviving screen sets then enter color testing via film and off-press color proofs. (In most test protocols, three-screen combinations are searched and tested first. The fourth screen is added when the survivors enter color testing.) The screen sets that pass the proofing tests graduate to press testing, where extensive halftone dot shape trials may also be conducted. The press testing stage may involve significant expense. Field testing and follow-up, with ongoing fine tuning as needed, form part of a long-term quality program.

Confronted with the expense of testing, developers may be tempted to skip it. Those who are mathematically sophisticated may justify the omission of tests by performing extra calculations to prove that their candidate screen sets are good ones, based on screen angle and screen frequency numbers alone.

This ignores some messy realities. First, a reliably predictive screen-combination theory is more elusive than the math suggests. Competing theoretical models are still being developed. Second (as shown in Chapter Three), the mathematical perfection of Cartesian space does not extend into the physical world where screen sets actually function. Unpredictable—often subtle—physical effects intrude. Finally, most ink-on-paper effects, especially those related to halftone dot shape, are not predicted by search tools.

Testing a screen set verifies that it is as moiré-free as a given search tool indicates and that it works when ink hits paper. Don't skip the testing phase before incorporating screen sets into products or using screen sets in real-world production circumstances.

Screen sets versus screen technology

When examining a printed color image, a good screen developer can see the respective visual effects of the screen set and the underlying screening technology. For anyone else it's difficult to separate the two. This confusion is sometimes encouraged: in promotional comparisons of screening methods, a single color image often represents an entire screening technology.

The appearance of any printed process-color image relies on both the underlying screening technology and the screen set used during imagesetting (Figure 9.1). An ill-chosen screen set can spoil any image. Any good screening technology makes it possible to develop and use good screen sets. However, no current screening technology guarantees that all possible screen sets will be good ones.

Screen set quality and variety is steadily improving as PostScript language screen set development emerges from its infancy.

What makes a good screen set?

The public doesn't think about screen sets or care about elegant theories that say certain screen sets will work. All that matters in the final analysis is how the image looks. Here's a summary of qualities that distinguish a good screen set:

- *Invisibility at any given screen frequency:* the screen should be as invisible as possible. At 150 LPI and above, the viewer shouldn't notice the screen set unless professionally interested in halftoning. In many screen sets, minor textures occur in various colors and tones. Such texturing should be unobtrusive, or absent. (As screen frequency increases, so does screen invisibility. Minor textures tend to scale down along with the screen period, so they also become less visible.)

- *Color consistency:* there should be no visible moiré patterns or long-period moiré effects such as rosette shifts and color shifts. At a wide range of inking levels (the entire range that can be anticipated in real press runs), the screen should remain free of moiré patterns and screen-related color shifts.
- *Tone reproduction and tonal smoothness:* highlights, midtones, and shadows should all reproduce well without heroic efforts on the part of the press operator or the electronic retoucher. The screen set should reproduce all tones and tonal transitions evenly, unless there is a specific reason to do otherwise.
- *Detail:* images should not suffer significant loss of detail in the screening process. (The whole production process tends to soften image detail, however.)

Method

Proprietary means of building supercell screen, built into the RIP.
Developed by halftone theorist and/or inventor.

Screen Set

C: 133.1 LPI, 15° + spot function
M: 133.1 LPI, 75° + spot function
Y: 143.7 LPI, 0° + spot function
K: 133.1 LPI, 45° + spot function
Developed by screen set engineering group.

Separation

Color-separated set of four films, output in sequence from imagesetter. Screen filter substitutes screen set for screen requested by user's application. Film output is used for proofing and printing.

FIGURE 9.1

A screening technology and its screen sets work together. Image quality depends on both. Screen sets thoroughly to make sure that users do not encounter costly screen problems on press runs.

Screen combination theories

There are various ways to combine four screens into a screen set. High-quality process color printing currently relies on the conventional rosette, which represents an unstable moiré-free state (as discussed in Chapter Four).

The conventional rosette provides good color stability in part because it has no repeating pattern of dot overlap. Due to the irrational-tangent angles used to create the rosette, the halftone dot-on-dot pattern never repeats itself within an image, even though it gives the illusion of a consistent rosette form. This lack of a repeating pattern makes the rosette relatively insensitive to color shifts due to registration errors.

Pixel-based digital screening systems, which can't create irrational-tangent angles, closely approximate the conventional rosette. This can work well, given the mathematical noise inherent in physical image-reproduction processes.

Approximating the irrational-tangent angles is only the first step; screens must be matched in angle offsets and frequency. Small deviations from the ideal angle or frequency can produce noticeable shifts of rosette form. The question for digital screen sets is: How do you determine the screens that superimpose well? Specifically, do you play by conventional rules or write your own—and if you write your own rules, what are they?

These questions are still being answered in the form of various mathematical models of screening. For screen set development with Adobe Accurate Screens software, three theoretical approaches have proven useful to date. All strive to create the conventional rosette.

1. Closely approximate the traditional screen assignments for cyan, magenta, and black, and vary the frequency of the yellow screen. This approach emulates irrational tangent screening systems. It works perfectly in theory if you get so close to 30-degree angle offsets and equal frequencies that the deviations are less than the mathematical noise of the image-reproduction process.

2. Cancel out variations from irrational tangent angles with complementary variations in the frequency of the 45-degree screen. This works perfectly in theory if you can also rotate the halftone cell "screen" within the supercell to fine-tune the screen frequency (a proprietary technique).

3. Use a combination of the above theories—aiming for perfection *and* compensating for deviations. This does not produce mathematical perfection, but it is practical and works well.

Basic recipe for conventional rosettes

The theoretical approaches just described begin with this screen set recipe:

- Assign the cyan, magenta, and black screens the same frequency.
- Assign the yellow screen a frequency about 8 percent higher than the other screens (multiply the other frequency by 1.08). This is not a critical factor; anything between 1.06 and 1.11 is worth investigating.
- Assign cyan to 15 degrees, magenta to 75 degrees, yellow to 0 degrees, and black to 45 degrees. The 15-degree and 75-degree angles are approximated closely; the 0- and 45-degree angles are exact.

Since the angle assignments are constant, you use frequency—often expressed to two decimal places—to specify a screen set. This defines the three initial screens. You specify the yellow later, after the initial screens have passed their first moiré tests on film.

The 15- and 75-degree (−15-degree) threshold arrays are mirror images of one another across the y axis. Given this, the screen matching is determined by just two characteristics: first, the difference between 15 degrees and the actual angle of the 15-degree screen; and second, the difference between the frequency of the 15-degree screen and the frequency of the (exactly) 45-degree screen. With approach 1 above, you try to minimize both of these errors. With approach 2, you try to compensate for angle error with a complementary frequency error. If you favor approach 3, you do a little of both.

Increasing yellow frequency

By increasing the frequency of the yellow screen, the basic screen set recipe departs from the conventional screen assignments. These call for four halftone screens of equal frequency, for the reasons explained in Chapter Four. The equal-frequency assumption is well entrenched in screening lore, and many trade shops still work with the traditional system, assigning the same frequency to all four screens.

Since when all four screens have the same frequency, the 15-degree moiré becomes a concern; screen swapping is often used in traditional screening to counteract this problem.

You should avoid screen sets where all four screens have the same frequency. By increasing the frequency of the yellow screen, you alter the grid patterns enough that the 15-degree moiré becomes invisible. Screen swaps are no longer needed, which greatly simplifies production, and computer-generated images—which often include both light greens and light oranges—look much better.

If you encounter an extraordinary situation where a 15-degree moiré pattern emerges and you can't control it by careful press work, you can try swapping screens, but it's better to redesign the screen set. Try varying the increase in the yellow frequency using factors from 1.06 to 1.11. As this book is being written, no 15-degree moiré has occurred with yellow at 108 percent.

Quality criteria for conventional rosettes

If the moiré period of a screen set exceeds eight times the length of the diagonal of an image, no significant rosette shift is likely within that image. Some screen sets created with Adobe Accurate Screens software provide very long moiré periods, and these form the basis for high-quality screening.

Using the basic recipe with Adobe Accurate Screens software, screen sets with deviations of ±0.0004 degree from 15 degrees and ±0.002 LPI between the 45- and 15-degree screens should have no visible moiré patterns and a stable rosette over a 40-inch-wide press sheet. The theoretical moiré period for such a screen set is between 10 feet and 0.5 mile, depending on which theory you consult, the screen frequency, and how the angle and frequency errors fall. In practice, a slight rosette shift may be present over a large press sheet in screen sets of 200 LPI and over, but this shift is probably less significant than the registration error of the finest presses.

Screen sets of this quality are uncommon and may not fall near the traditional frequency numbers. To find high-quality screen sets at the screen space you are using, you may have to deviate from your desired frequency. As screen frequency increases, screen sets become less plentiful, so for screen sets in high-frequency ranges you may need to increase screen space.

Another option is to accept a small amount of rosette shift. Many production settings do not require screen sets that meet the highest quality standards; more screen sets are available if you relax your quality standards slightly; and for smaller images or less-than-precise presses, these screen sets can give perfectly good results.

The importance of spot functions

Once the basic rosette criteria are satisfied, dot shape is critical to screen set quality. Given the number of dot shapes, their various production applications, and the ease with which you can create them with the PostScript language, the spot function may be the argument you explore most in your screen set development.

The spot function can't make a screen set, but it can break it. Ink-on-paper effects, especially dot join and shadow behavior, influence the tonal reproduction of different images in different ways. A skillful user of screen sets chooses different halftone dot shapes based on this tonal behavior—if the behavior is predictable. Such predictability is based on press tests.

Consult Chapter Five and the Bibliography for further information about spot functions and dot shape.

Screen filters

When users specify screens directly, as they do in PPD files or applications such as Adobe Photoshop, they can request untested screen sets. Given the importance of using well tested screen sets, a means of delivering only proven sets is needed.

For this reason many screen developers incorporate their proven screen sets into a *screen filter* (Figure 9.2). A screen filter intercepts calls to **setscreen** and **setcolorscreen**, substituting proven screen set values for the requested screen set. This makes the screening transparent to the user and protects users from arbitrary or ill-considered screen set choices (even their own). Most screen filters can be disabled to allow direct access to **setscreen** or **setcolorscreen**.

A basic screen filter program is available in Appendix C.

UCR, GCR, and varying the black angle

The basic screen set recipe assigns the black screen to 45 degrees. This is because black shows a screen most strongly, and screens are least apparent at 45 degrees. As long as your images have a significant amount of intermediate tonal value in the black screen, assigning black to 45 degrees makes sense.

In four-color production using UCR (undercolor removal), it's possible to have images in which the black screen has few tone values outside of shadow areas. A user may not want to waste the premium 45-degree angle on a scanty black screen. If you provide screen set choices for use with UCR, it's advisable to permit users to assign the 45-degree angle to cyan or magenta, depending on the nature of the image.

GCR (gray component replacement) locates tonal values more continuously throughout the black screen. GCR can be applied in various amounts, usually expressed in percentage terms. A high percentage of GCR can produce a color separation with full-range black—the black plate looks almost like a black-and-white photo. Obviously you would want to assign the black screen to 45 degrees in such a case. A full-range black separation generally corresponds to a heavy GCR setting of 80 to 100 percent. Full-range black requires vigilant press work, so less GCR is usually used; a common starting range is 60 to 70 percent. This provides an ample amount of black screen, and still justifies the assignment of black to 45 degrees in most circumstances.

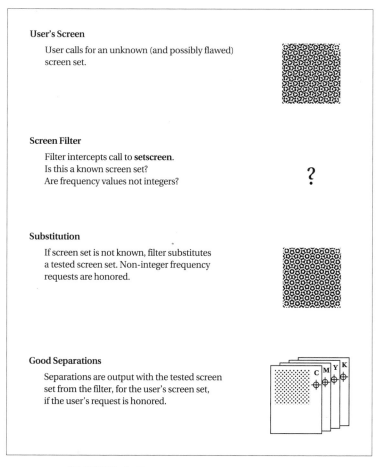

User's Screen

> User calls for an unknown (and possibly flawed) screen set.

Screen Filter

> Filter intercepts call to **setscreen**.
> Is this a known screen set?
> Are frequency values not integers?

Substitution

> If screen set is not known, filter substitutes a tested screen set. Non-integer frequency requests are honored.

Good Separations

> Separations are output with the tested screen set from the filter, for the user's screen set, if the user's request is honored.

FIGURE 9.2

*A screen filter is downloaded to the RIP, redefining the **setscreen** operator. Known screen sets are listed in the filter. Tested screen sets are substituted for integer screen calls.*

Traditional frequencies

A set of familiar frequency numbers has become established in the printing trade. Typically these are 85, 100, 110, 120, 133, 150, 175, and 200 LPI. Trade clients tend be uneasy about screening in general, since screening failures often appear on press with expensive implications. To avoid ruffling clients, the familiar LPI numbers continue to be used despite the fact that frequency disparities usually occur with digital screening systems. For example, a so-called 150 LPI screen might actually be 152.74 LPI.

Given the relative scarcity of the best screen sets, you may encounter a situation in which an excellent screen set—at 142.67 LPI, say—does not fall near the familiar frequency comfort zones and no good alternative screen set falls closer. If you decide to use the excellent screen set, you have to label it for public consumption. Since printing equipment is rated according to the half-tone screen fineness it can reliably print, a 5 LPI difference between nominal and actual frequency seems a prudent limit.

Rotated angle sets

All output devices have a certain amount of vibration or "jitter" in their imaging mechanisms. On some devices this jitter has a magnitude or character that interferes with the screens, producing artifacts. One common solution is to rotate the entire set of angle assignments. This requires substantial experimentation and makes the searching and testing of screen sets more involved. The exact 0- and 45-degree angles probably can't be used in a rotated set, and you are less likely to have a handy mirror-image pair of screens such as the 15- and 75-degree screens.

Implications of high frequency screening

In the current print-production culture, high-frequency screens (175 LPI and above) are often considered superior. Only the finer printers use high-frequency screens, for they are tricky to print and demand excellent, carefully maintained presses and prepress production equipment. Relative to other screens, high-frequency screens are less visible and show more detail. They also have higher dot gain, so production is more difficult. It's an accomplishment to use high-frequency screens well, and those who do so are generally proud of it.

You will probably find far more day-to-day use for your screen sets in the 133 LPI and 150 LPI vicinities than for the your screen sets in the 200 LPI and up range. In any frequency range, however, as frequency increases you need to pay special attention to dot gain, tonal contouring, and visible artifacts.

Dot gain becomes progressively more important as frequency increases. Above 200 LPI, dot-gain management makes printing a challenge. Aside from the increased amount of dot edge in all screens as frequency increases, dot gain takes on a new dimension starting at about 150 LPI, at which point optical dot gain becomes significant, in addition to mechanical dot gain. As dot gain increases, shadows tend to plug up also. Thus, high-frequency screens should have dot shapes that don't exacerbate dot gain. A spot function that creates round highlight dots, inverted round shadow dots, and slightly elliptical midtone transition dots is a good starting point for development of such screens.

As frequency rises, the number of pixels in the halftone cell falls. Once the LPI rises above the number given by the resolution divided by 16, the halftone cell no longer has enough pixels to render the full 256-gray tonal range of the

PostScript language. (For example, for 256 pixels in the cell, a 200 LPI screen requires an imagesetter resolution of at least 3200 dpi.) Subtle tonal contouring shows up at 200 grays or so, and becomes clearly visible to the practiced eye at about 150 grays. If the image is textured or "noisy," you can get away with fewer grays before contouring becomes objectionable.

You may need to design screen sets at screen frequencies that result in fewer than 256 pixels per halftone cell. This produces tonal contouring. Mixing noise into a halftone is a well-known technique for producing smoother gray transitions in such situations. This technique is used by the PixelBurst coprocessor, which applies a random diffusion to the values in the threshold array. Adobe Accurate Screens software does not mix noise into the halftone, but the distortions of the halftone cell shapes within the supertile produces smoother looking tonal transitions than are delivered by equivalent screens produced with the standard PostScript RT Screening.

As the number of pixels in the halftone cell falls, the RIP's options in constructing the supercell become limited, making cell balancing difficult. This can lead to a textured or grid-like artifact in some screens. Such artifacts, if they appear, are most visible in smooth tints. The visibility of the artifacts varies greatly from screen to screen. Similar effects can occur with other supercell screening methods.

Low-resolution, high-frequency screen set development should proceed with care to avoid incorporating screens with artifacts into screen sets. Many supercell screens show slight artifact patterns in films viewed on a light table, but these patterns vanish when the same films are printed. Run press tests if in doubt.

As imagesetter resolution decreases, device pixels grow in size, eventually approaching a size that the printing process can consistently resolve. Once this point is reached, artifacts may become visible on press sheets. This varies with printing method, ink, paper, and printing. In offset lithography—the most widely used printing method—physical features on the film that fall below 12 microns in diameter are not consistently printed. A well-formed pixel from a 2000 dpi imagesetter is approximately this size. At higher image-setter resolutions current printing methods can't consistently resolve pixel-size features even if they are present on the film.

Selecting Screen Sets

Screen sets are device-specific. A given screen set resides in an output device and relies on the halftone screen behavior of that device. Although identical screen sets may function well in different devices, each screen set must be tested with each device individually.

This chapter and the next outline a methodology for identifying and testing screen sets created with Adobe Accurate Screens technology. Both chapters assume you are familiar with the topics presented so far in this book.

The discussion is based on the basic screen set recipe described in Chapter Nine. If you plan to use another screen combination approach (perhaps one that incorporates a theory you have developed) you need to consider the issues discussed here, even if they lead you to different conclusions.

In the selection stage of development, you identify candidate screen sets and qualify the most promising ones. This chapter focuses on developing screen sets for use in printing color-separated images using the four standard process colors: cyan, magenta, yellow, and black.

You may choose a less rigorous development process than the methodology given here. In doing so, however, you pass significant risks along to your users, who may not be willing to accept the consequences in their day-to-day commercial activities. Some screen sets perform consistently well, both in preliminary press tests and in a wide range of real-world production situations in the field. Other screen sets perform well in preliminary tests but inconsistently in the field. The development methodology assumes that this may happen, and provides for ongoing screen set upgrades and improvements.

Establishing screen set criteria

Since every screen set functions in a specific imaging environment, the first task is to set quality criteria appropriate to the intended environment. Several considerations enter into the assessment:

- What is the size of the largest likely color image? Are color images in constant use in the intended market or only used occasionally? What is the typical content of the images to be halftoned? Do the typical images require, or can they benefit from, moiré-free screen sets? If so, how much rosette shift can be tolerated?
- What level of quality do users (and the readers they serve) expect? Is this expectation likely to change during the lifetime of the screen sets? ·
- Given the mechanical and optical behavior of the output device, how accurate a halftone screen set can it reproduce?
- Can a high degree of screen accuracy be maintained by the anticipated users' prepress production methods?
- Can a high degree of screen accuracy be maintained by the anticipated users' printing methods? What types of paper stock will be used?

The answers to the above questions set standards for the screen sets you plan to develop. The next step is to establish the specifics for each screen set.

- Establish the frequency range. For example, typical screen sets on a device with both 1200 dpi and 2400 dpi settings might be centered at 85, 100, 120, 133, 150, 175, and 200 LPI, all with a ±5 LPI range.
- Determine the desired moiré and rosette character. Is the absence of visible moiré patterns good enough for your application, or do you need a rosette structure so stable that it has no detectable shift across the diagonal of the largest anticipated image? If an absence of visible patterns is sufficient, you have a greater choice of candidate screen sets.
- Determine screen space. If only the highest-rated screen sets will do, you may need to increase screen space on a PostScript Level 1 imagesetter or **MaxScreenStorage** on a PostScript Level 2 imagesetter.
- Establish the necessary dot shapes. If you plan to offer the best possible screen sets, chances are you will also offer a selection of dot shapes. Decide how many to offer—you need to test each one when you reach the press-testing stage.

Identifying candidate screen sets

Using the search program in Appendix A, other search programs, or a program of your own design, search for candidate screen sets in your chosen frequency ranges. Many screen sets are available. A search program provides you with information you need to evaluate screen set quality *from the viewpoint of the screen combination theory used to write the search program*. The program in Appendix A is based on the traditional screen recipe, and has produced good results. Search programs based on other theories may offer different screen sets.

The search program in Appendix A queries a PostScript Level 1 Adobe Accurate Screens RIP using the **checkscreen** operator. Searches take time and tend to tie up expensive hardware. If you are comfortable with trigonometry and screen theory and can program in the PostScript language, you can write a search program that operates on a PostScript language laser printer by modeling supercell outlines and comparing the resulting screens with one another. You can also write such programs in other computer languages.

Once a search report is generated, analyzing it to select candidate screen sets takes only a few minutes. You usually select by a quality index. Also review the specific frequency and angle numbers as you examine candidate sets. You can learn this way, and may notice trends that bear investigation.

Search programs only give you frequency and angle information related to moiré and rosette formation. The dot shapes are up to you. You can write a spot function test program that uses synthetic data and the PostScript language **image** operator (refer to the *PostScript Language Program Design*). Try spot functions on a PostScript laser printer and modify them until they produce the desired halftone dot at every point in the tone range.

Calibrating the output chain

For reasons discussed in Chapter Three, the imagesetting output chain—RIP, recorder (electronics, optics, and mechanical transport), film, processor, and chemistry—must be stable to provide good film for high-quality color. Adjusting and stabilizing the imagesetting equipment and establishing a highly stable laboratory environment is ideal for the development of high-quality screen sets. Development work in a production environment requires a very stable imagesetting chain.

Films for high-quality color printing can tolerate very little variation among the four color-separated films. Such variation causes errors in the finished job. Thus, to evaluate screen sets for high-quality printing you must operate within the tightest production tolerances in your laboratory.

Film appropriate for color production must be dimensionally consistent; it should fall well within the manufacturer's dimensionality tolerances (certain types of equipment are not suitable for color work because they allow too much dimensional variation). A register error of ±0.001 inch between films can throw color jobs out of tolerance on the stripping table, and can throw the traps off in trapped images. For example, one guideline for high-quality sheet-fed printing calls for errors to be held within ±0.002 inch in trapping, ±0.001 inch in stripping, and ±0.001 inch on press.

Film appropriate for color production must also be consistent in tonal value; a global variation of ±3 percent in tonal value at the midtone dot is tolerated, but the film-to-film variation must be much less than this. A variation of more than ±1 percent between films in a given separation can produce noticeable color shifts in images with grays or low-saturation colors.

To keep variations to a minimum, experienced imagesetter operators run all films in a color separation at one time and never change film or chemistry in the middle of a separation. This greatly improves consistency and should be your standard practice in developing screen sets.

Tonal calibration is a day-to-day activity. It takes a while for a calibration routine to settle in with equipment, materials, and staff, so it's a good idea to start it well before you need it. This way, when you need accurate color separations, you'll be able to generate them.

Calibration software provides test pages. At minimum you should perform a daily calibration check, filing the test page and keeping the readings for statistical and historical analysis. When you begin calibration, it's a good idea to perform more frequent checks until you understand how your system operates.

A test page should include dimensional stability targets, known gray tints for tonal-response monitoring, a gray ramp, and perhaps microline targets and large tint areas. Such test pages are available commercially. You may prefer to program your own test page. If you do this within a graphics application, make sure you linearize any transfer-function operations that your application or its related PPD files perform.

Moiré and rosette behavior

A direct, simple way to evaluate a screen set for moiré and rosette behavior is to image the individual screens on positive films as a flat tint of about 30 percent gray. This tint is imaged on three films corresponding to the cyan, magenta, and black screens. The individual films are examined for even tone and then superimposed in register on a light table to examine the rosettes. When imaged as a film positive, 30 percent gray provides dots that are big enough to form clear rosettes, yet small enough to provide plenty of open space, so you can see the dots on the other two films.

A PostScript test page for this activity is available in Appendix B. The test page is scaleable, so you can easily adjust it to the maximum page size you need. It is advisable to use a PostScript language test page so you can easily adjust the requested screen angles, screen frequencies, and spot functions.

Imaging a large, perfectly smooth, flat tint is a tough test. The slightest flaw shows up readily in the large area of even tone. When a screen passes this test, you can be confident that your equipment is in good mechanical order. Before running tests with new candidate screen sets, image a screen set that you know produces good results. Do this daily as a control. After verifying that the equipment images the control screen set well, store the day's control for long-term analysis of your equipment's drift.

To run a test, adjust the test page size to produce either the largest image your output device can support, or the largest image for which you are developing the screen set. Insert the screen frequencies, angles, and spot functions of the three screens to be tested where indicated in the test page file, and imageset the file. Process the film and examine it on a good-quality light table. If the tint area is perfectly smooth on the individual films, put all three films down in register.

On inexpensive light boxes, which often run hot, it may be difficult to accurately register the three films due to unequal thermal expansion of the film base. For serious screen set development, use a professional light table, which runs cool.

Once the films are positioned on the light table, test for gross moiré by looking into the image area. If the screen set is free of visible moiré, you will feel as if you are looking into a pool of perfectly even tone, with no perceptible tone shifts at any point in the entire image area. If this is not the case, and if you can verify that the films themselves are in excellent register, you must decide whether to reject the screen set or to check your equipment by running a known screen set.

Assuming the screen set passes the visual check for gross moiré, you can examine the rosette structure with a loupe (usually about 20 power is best). You may want to position the top film to create the rosette form you prefer. Your goal is rosette *stability*—once the films are down, you hope to see the same rosette over the entire image. Remember that a severe rosette shift is the same as a visible moiré pattern. As the moiré period becomes longer the visible moiré disappears, but the shifting may remain visible under a loupe as changes in rosette form. Examine widely spaced areas of the image for shifts in rosette form.

Ideally, you see a perfectly consistent rosette structure over the whole image. This indicates essentially no visible moiré: an infinitely long moiré period. Such a screen set is a gem.

More often, you see some shifting of rosette forms, indicative of a long-period moiré (much longer than the diagonal of the image test area, or it would have shown up as a visible tone shift). When you detect such shifting, decide if the shift is minor enough that the screen set still meets your quality requirements. A shift of one-half the distance between halftone dots changes the rosette form completely. Eliminate screen sets that show a shift of more than one-eighth of a dot over the long diagonal of the tint area.

Other factors may influence your decision: How good are your other candidate sets? Do you have another candidate set in the same frequency range that appears more stable? If not, you may have to increase screen space or accept a screen set with slightly shifting rosettes.

You rarely achieve perfectly consistent rosette forms over an entire press sheet, due to the normal variations and nonlinearities of the printing process. For all but the most picky (and perhaps unrealistic) printing clients, a slight shift in rosette form causes no problem even in high-quality printing.

When you are satisfied with the basic three-screen screen set, place the fourth (yellow) tint page—0 degrees and 108 percent of the other frequency—in register with the other films. Now when you examine the screen set from a distance of about 18 inches with the unaided eye, a slightly confused or "soap-suds" pattern appears. Compare this with the strong patterns that emerge when a fourth screen of the same frequency is placed in register over the other three screens (one trial with one screen set will suffice to show you what this looks like).

Varying the frequency of the fourth screen assumes that users will employ it for yellow. If other colors are used with this screen, the results are unpredictable.

Spot function offsets

A screen set should start with rosette forms that will give clear-centered rosettes in the finished image. Since dot-centered rosettes and clear-centered rosettes are symmetrically opposite forms, dot-centered rosettes on a negative give clear-centered rosettes on a press sheet. You can use PostScript code to fine tune the position of halftone dots via a spot-function offset to align the screens in your screen sets for optimum rosette form. It is advisable to perform such fine tuning early in the development process, as certain spot function offsets can interact unpredictably with the supercell cell-balancing process. Examine your fine-tuned screens for artifacts before proceeding.

Evaluating for dot structure

Once the moiré and rosette evaluations are complete, it's time to evaluate the halftone dot. Since dot structure varies in a supercell-based system, the dots show a variety of outlines even in areas of the same gray. Your task is to determine whether the spot function, spot function offsets, and supercell calculation produce halftone dots that meet your expectations.

You need to evaluate areas of even tone over the entire gray range, and also areas of constantly changing tone. Your standard calibration test page, with tint targets and gray ramp, is an appropriate test vehicle.

Imageset each screen in the screen set using the test page file, and process the film. Then evaluate dot structure with a high-power loupe (50 power is ideal). Some imagesetters can image individual pixels with total clarity, while others image individual pixels as hazy areas on the film.

First, check spot function performance. Is the dot shape what you desired? It's easy to get carried away looking at moiré, rosette, and pixel characteristics, and miss the fact that the dots aren't quite the right shape because you entered the spot function wrong! Verify that the overall dot design is what you intend.

Next, examine the gray ramp for gross artifacts. These show up as a fine grid-like or fabric-like texture in certain tonal ranges of single film pages. The effect appears at the same tonal location every time you image the specific screen. If such artifacts are present, ask yourself if they are pronounced enough to survive the printing process. Often a slight texturing is visible but not significant, as it disappears completely in printing. (This is especially true for the yellow screen.) If the screen set is otherwise excellent, print samples of the individual screens to settle any doubts. Artifacts are likely to vary from screen to screen within the same screen set, since they are specific to different supercells (the 15- and 75-degree screens are built on mirror images of the same supercell). As mentioned earlier, you are more likely to encounter artifacts with small halftone cells.

Finally, if your output device can clearly image individual pixels, examine both the solid tints and the gray ramp to determine whether the dot edges are within your quality range. For resolutions above 2000 dpi this is primarily a cosmetic issue. If the dots show unacceptable forms at lower resolutions (where the halftone cells become quite small), try modifying your spot function, or develop another spot function that produces the desired dot.

Occasional isolated pixels or small hooks on isolated dots at high resolution will not impair the printed images and often improve tonal smoothness. At resolutions above about 2000 dpi the printing process can't resolve such artifacts.

Contouring at extremes of tone range

As you examine the gray ramp you should observe no obvious gray-level contouring shade-stepping in the tones, unless your halftone cell has fewer than 150 pixels. There is one important exception: you usually observe contouring at the darkest extremes of the gray ramp when examining film on a light table or light box. In this very dark area the last few pixels are being turned off as the halftone dot shrinks first to a tiny pinhole and then to nothing, so the relative changes in illumination become very large as three, two, and finally one pixel are all that is left to emit light through the film. The eye readily perceives the changes in illumination levels when viewing on a light table, but at high resolution the pixels are so small that they are not resolved by the printing process. Also, on a negative they represent the tiniest highlight dots, not the darkest shadows. This type of shade stepping is rarely a problem in the final printed image.

The PixelBurst coprocessor offers an error-diffusion option that reduces visible contouring due to small halftone cells.

One-color screens

Most one-color imagesetting jobs use the 45-degree screen of the screen set nearest the requested frequency. However, if you are producing single screens specifically for one-color printing, these should be tested if they incorporate new spot functions. Such screens need not use Adobe Accurate Screens software, although they may deliver smoother tone reproduction if they do. Unless a special effect is intended, assign them a screen angle of 45 degrees. The screen frequency is not critical; it can vary by ±3 LPI.

On to color testing

If your screen sets meet your quality criteria, you can progress to testing with color images, as covered in the next chapter. Otherwise, you need to try other screen sets, or perhaps increase screen space and start a new search.

Press Testing and the Long Term

Once a screen set has satisfied your quality criteria on film, it's time to begin testing and development with color press testing. Screen sets that perform well on press are candidates for incorporation into screen filters and distribution.

Avoid substituting off-press color proofs for press testing. Although off-press color proofing is essential in production, it's not possible to evaluate certain ink-related dot behavior accurately on an off-press color proof, even a very good one. Such proofs simulate dot gain, but true dot-gain and dot-join behavior varies with ink, paper, and press conditions. *Screen sets seldom fail at the off-press proofing stage if they have passed a rigorous film-testing protocol. It's on press that the next serious test occurs.*

The wide range of production conditions in the field tests a screen set far more thoroughly than you can in a development program, even a thorough one. Shortly after release of your screen sets, you have information about how they perform in the field. In the final stage of development, you make use of this valuable information to fine-tune your screen sets and build an experience base that you can pass along to your users.

This chapter assumes you are running your screen set tests on a lithographic offset color press with at least four units, possibly a color proofing press. If you are producing screen sets for other printing methods, most of this chapter still holds true.

Adopting a test suite

Testing should always be performed with standard subject material. When testing on film, it's taken for granted that a test page will be adopted. When it's time to test in color, however, various temptations arise. Given the cost of testing from this point on, you may be offered a variety of images to use without consideration of the technical merits. If you test screen sets with a selection of differing images you will have little objective data to compare, and your confidence in your screen sets will be less than it should be.

Ideally, your test suite represents the standard by which you measure one screen set against another. With the test suite you obtain objective information over an extended period of time. While there is no law stating that test images must be unattractive, whether they are "pleasing" is of little quantitative concern.

In addition to the images, you need a set of standard color quality-control test targets to make the quantitative measurements. For each test you need to verify that the printing plates and press sheets are produced within your tolerances. This is usually accomplished by double-burning the targets onto the test plates. There are several sets of commercial test targets available for these purposes.

For extensive testing, purchase a set of quality-control targets for your printer to use in your tests exclusively. This is expensive, but it minimizes data drift due to wear and tear on the printer's targets, which take a day-to-day beating.

You should incorporate a standard test object on all of your films too, if your software doesn't already do this. A set of tint targets in 10 percent steps is the minimum, along with a tone ramp to check dot formation and shade stepping. These targets should be identical from film to film in your color separations (there should be no gray-balance adjustments within these targets, for example).

Test form specification

The following is a PostScript test form specification for images and image characteristics to include in the test form or forms that comprise your test suite. The specification was developed by a joint task force sponsored by the Graphic Communication Association (GCA) and Adobe Systems Incorporated.

Targets should be identical on each form. Design each form so that you have the same data available whether the form runs through the press horizontally or vertically. You can use one test form that is a large composite image made up of several elements, or you can use several forms. These items should appear on each form:

- Registration targets in the corners and center of the test suite, to allow you to accurately measure register error on the press sheets.
- A hairline rule in the form of a square box around the perimeter of the image, to establish squareness and register error at the edge of the press sheet (it is very difficult to hold such a rule in perfect register during printing). You may wish to place the above registration targets at the corners of this box.

128

- A tint comparator for color balance, to allow you to detect color shifts that occur on press. This comparator's percentages depend on the inks used, but a general-purpose comparator consists of a wide column of 3-color black (50 percent cyan, 39 percent magenta, 39 percent yellow) surrounding a narrow column of a 65 percent black tint. When color balance is correct, both the three-color black and the 65 percent black tint appear identical. This target is very sensitive to color shift.
- Tint targets in 5 percent steps for each color, plus 2 percent and 98 percent, and possibly also 3 percent and 97 percent, depending on the quality level for which your screen sets are intended. (Make the individual tint blocks at least 5 mm square to allow adequate room to take densitometer readings.)

If you have more than one form, the following items need not be repeated on each form:

- Nine different color tone ramps to show moiré and rosette-formation problems. These are cyan, magenta, yellow, black, red (magenta and yellow), blue (cyan and magenta), green (cyan and yellow), three-color black (cyan, magenta and yellow), and four-color black. No color balance should be attempted; all colors in all ramps run equally from 0 to 100 percent. These ramps also establish whether artifacts that appear on the film appear on the press sheet.
- Individual images, both computer-generated artwork and natural photos, containing the type of material for which your screen set will be used. You may include high-key, low-key, high-contrast and low-contrast images, as well as flesh tones, fluorescent colors, fabrics, four-color black-and-white (quad-tones), duotones, saturated colors, edge-of-gamut colors, and so forth. Rarely do all of these categories of images end up on a single test form, yet any given screen set is likely to reproduce some categories better than others.

Your printer should also burn the previously mentioned standard color quality control test targets (your own if possible) onto the plates for all press tests. Press runs are monitored with these targets using the printer's normal quality-control methods. The quality-control targets should include at least the standard set of tints, overprints, and slur targets, but if you are performing high-quality testing they should also include exposure targets, micro-resolution targets, dot-gain targets, and other targets you believe will give meaningful data. See the Bibliography for more information.

The test suite provides consistent input for testing, measurement, interpretation, and statistical analysis. Measuring the various test targets, you confirm that press sheets are comparable before making visual comparisons of the images on the sheets. Once your test suite is chosen, it should remain constant for the duration of your testing and development cycle. This ensures comparable results over the long term.

Additionally, images must remain constant for reliable visual comparisons of screening effects. If the color or content of the test images changes, it is difficult for viewers to make objective comparisons of the screens.

Once established, test suites—being a constant point of reference—almost immediately become the focal point of performance tests that measure system imaging speed. Such use has no direct impact on screen set testing, unless the performance testing and screen set imaging take place simultaneously. If the needs of performance tests are such that methodical screen set testing is jeopardized, do the screen set testing at another time.

Preparing for the press test

Once a test suite is established and proofed to your satisfaction with a known screen set, conduct a press test to establish an initial set of baseline values with a known screen set. As testing progresses this baseline becomes better established statistically.

A separate form is output for each screen set. Measure the resulting film separations with a properly calibrated transmission densitometer to ensure that the tonal values and densities are within tolerance. Examine the films visually with both a loupe and the unaided eye to ensure that the screen set behaved as you expected given the results of your earlier film tests.

If you make color proofs, measure the quality-control targets on the proof, evaluate the proof visually, and file both the proof and the readings for later reference. The usual purpose of color proofing is to establish color before going to press and discover gross moiré patterns or trapping problems that may have escaped notice at earlier stages. For your testing, where the same images are used over and over, it isn't necessary to incur the constant expense of color proofing to repeatedly check the known color of the test suite. Once you have settled on the color (after an initial series of color proofs) you can rely on visual film checks and measurement of tint targets before going to press. Although a color-dependent moiré pattern could escape detection during film testing and show up on a color proof, you would catch it in the press tests, so it's difficult to justify the expense of proofing known color.

Select a single, stable printing facility as your primary printer for all your tests. While your screen sets have to perform under a variety of printing circumstances, your initial tests must be conducted under stable circumstances. In addition, a good printer can teach you many practical things about the production process if you develop a good working relationship. Once your screen sets pass your initial press tests, you can test them with other printing sites.

Plates and paper

Films are stripped into flats and used to make printing plates. (In cases where you produce composite film and need no stripping, a flat should be made anyway to include the necessary targets.) Printing-plate exposure is critical. Most printers, being aware of this, take care to give the proper exposure, but variations do occur. Specify that the printer use a suitable plate exposure measurement target. Also specify that the plates be measured after they are made, to verify that exposure and dot gain (or dot loss if the plates are positive-working) are within a reasonable tolerance you have established for the test. Determine this tolerance by discussion with the printer.

Select paper stock that is both appropriate and likely to remain available. Since paper stocks are discontinued occasionally, choose stock with common characteristics. Your printer is likely to have a house proofing stock that meets these requirements and runs well on the printer's equipment. If you choose another stock, do so with the printer's involvement, and expect to invest time, effort, and expense as the printer learns how to run the new stock consistently.

Press test

Once on press, adjust the press to accurately reproduce the targets, not the images. On commercial presses, the press operators may have to be reminded of this. Their normal priorities are to make the images look good first, and to use the targets only as a means to this end. Good proofing-press operators, on the other hand, run to the targets. The press operator should take frequent color reflection densitometer readings of the ink density while the press is brought up to color and during the run.

Establish a set of target ink densities for your press runs. Often the SWOP standard (Specifications for Web Offset Publications) is assumed to be the ideal in these circumstances, though it may not be ideal for your tests. The SWOP standard is well established and generally known, but is designed for use with web offset publications: magazines and catalogs for the most part. The SWOP standard calls for specific inks, a specific range of ink densities, and dot gains which are based, among other things, on 133 LPI screens (higher screen frequencies can be used by agreement). If you are developing screen sets for use in circumstances that have little or nothing to do with magazines or catalogs, you might be better off working to another standard or developing a standard of your own.

A screen set test is more involved than a typical press-proofing run. Once you get the press up to color, run a set of press sheets at your target densities. Then pull a progressive proof so you can easily evaluate individual colors. A partial progressive proof consisting of individual sheets of cyan, magenta, yellow, and black plus a sheet of cyan, magenta, and yellow should suffice for most testing. For really detailed examination, get a complete progressive proof. You may decide that complete progressive proofs aren't always needed.

Once you've pulled the progressive proof, return to four-color press sheets and vary the inking. Pull the ink densities down and push them up to see how your screen set performs under conditions beyond those encountered in regular practice. Have the press operators make notations on the press sheets, recording their ink density readings.

Then change paper stock and repeat the process, keeping in mind that you can change stock just so far before the dot gain falls outside the range for which your color was originally adjusted. For drastic changes in paper stock you have to run a separate test, using a test suite that has the correct dot gain compensation.

Finally, try throwing the press out of adjustment to emulate common things that can go wrong. This makes many press operators uneasy, and for a proofing press it can be risky if taken too far. If you are familiar with offset printing, suggest various common printing disasters. Once over the initial reticence, the press operator will probably suggest other typical disasters you can mimic. Be sure to make accurate notations on the press sheets. This is not only for evaluation, but so you can try the same scenarios on other tests (you are unlikely to exactly duplicate the same "bad" condition on subsequent tests, so you can't be very fussy about this). Don't push the press operator about misadjusting the press; it can make it difficult to put things right for the next customer's job.

Work area and tools for evaluation

Once the test press sheets are dried and delivered, you can evaluate them. For this you need a large amount of table or counter space so you can spread out various press sheets for side-by-side comparisons. Ideally this work area should have 5000°K lighting with a Color Rendering Index of 90 or better and should be painted a Munsell N8 gray or equivalent. Your printer should be able to tell you where to obtain the lights and paint in your area. For critical color viewing you also need a large viewing booth. These are available commercially, but again your printer or a local color trade shop can advise you on sources of local supply for materials to build your own (at much less cost) according to the ANSI Standard PH2.32 (1972). There are also ISO standards you can use for color viewing. For additional material on lighting and color viewing specifications, refer to the Bibliography.

You need a substantial amount of flat storage space to catalog and store press sheets for initial and long-term evaluation. This storage space tends to fill up fast. A large paper cutter may also come in handy.

To gather data from the press sheets for evaluation, you need a set of good loupes (10, 20, and 50 power are the basics), and a color reflection densitometer. Some modern color reflection densitometers can be connected to a small computer, allowing you to gather their data for statistical analysis or display.

Evaluation

Everyone eagerly looks at the press tests to see how the new screen set performs. This proves nothing without a standard. How well the does the new screen set perform in comparison with other screen sets? Before examining the new screen set's test suite side-by-side with a standard screen set's test suite, establish that the quality-control targets on the press sheets are comparable. Otherwise, a side-by-side comparison gives you unreliable information.

Check the targets visually, and also check the color reflection densitometer readings from the printing plant; or better yet, take another set of readings in your own laboratory. Readings are rarely identical on press sheets from different press runs, but they should be close enough that the press work can be considered equivalent. (You have to do some homework with the printer to establish a working tolerance for this determination.)

Essential qualifying measurements include: densitometer measurements of ink density of the four process colors, two-color overprints, and three-color overprints; densitometer measurement of dot gain at 25, 50, and 75 percent tone for each color; visual assessments of the nature of the dot gain (mechanical dot gain, optical dot gain, slur, or dot doubling); and visual comparisons of gray balance using the printers' gray-balance targets. Accurate register is necessary. If the paper stocks, inks, and images are reasonably identical (even the same paper and ink often shows batch variations), and if the measurements and visual assessments are reasonably close, a visual comparison is likely to be valid. How close is "reasonably close"? You have to decide this, based on your quality criteria, the needs of the intended users of the screen sets, and your own reading of the literature. (The SWOP standards, for instance, provide for an allowable deviation of ±0.07 density units from the standard IPA target densities, midtone dot gain of 24 percent ±4 percent from film to paper, accurate gray balance throughout the tone range, and ANSI or ISO standard viewing conditions.)

Don't forget to catalog the defective press sheets if you created some on the test. Most screen sets look good when superbly printed; can your screen set tolerate *mediocre* printing? This is the true test of day-to-day usefulness. Establish how the sheets are defective and how well the screen set tolerates the defects.

After establishing that the targets on the test and standard press sheets are objectively close enough to make side-by-side visual comparisons valid, proceed with subjective evaluations. You may want to use a quality scale so that numerous viewers can grade side-by-side sheets in a survey.

Then move to a more objective visual evaluation. This evaluation will vary, given your priorities. Here are some of the specific things to evaluate:

- Under what conditions, if any, did the screen set develop a visible moiré pattern? Were these conditions highly unusual, or were they the type of register, inking, or press errors that can happen easily? If a moiré pattern develops under common less-than-perfect printing conditions, the screen set is not robust enough for reliable use in the field.

- Does the screen set perform acceptably in all tone ranges, or at least in the tone ranges of special interest for the intended use? Is the tonal response smooth in the highlights and the midtone dot-join region? If you have designed the dot shape to provide a tonal break in a certain tone region, does the break show up where you want it? Shadow detail is especially sensitive to dot shape and is an area in which different screen sets are likely to show different behavior. A key quantitative test for shadow detail is print contrast—the higher the print contrast, the more open the shadows. Print contrast requires reflection density measurements of both solid and 75 percent tint targets. Using the simple formula

$$((D_{solid} - D75\%_{tint}) \div (D_{solid})) \times 100$$

  you can establish print contrast quantitatively for all four colors. A value of 25 percent or better is the target under SWOP standards. First establish print contrast for the press sheet using the density of the printer's 75 percent control targets, and then establish print contrast for your screen set using the density of a 75 percent tint in your screen set test suite.

- Screening artifacts include contouring (shade stepping), undesirable features on the individual films, and the formation of visible patterns in the superimposed screens. You should not see contouring and film artifacts on the press sheets, though they are usually present on the film. Ideally, there is no visible patterning, but some often occurs in the lighter shadow colors. (Recall that a small amount of patterning occurs frequently in printed pieces as a matter of course, and is often minimized by printing at higher frequency.)

Depending on the design of your screen set and its intended use, you may want to evaluate other screen characteristics for their sensitivity to prepress production errors and printing conditions. After evaluation, catalog the observations and measurements and carefully file the press sheets from each test for future reference. This will be key data you can use to revise or review the screen set later.

Releasing screen sets

After you become confident that a screen set performs well you can distribute it by various means, preferably first to a selected set of beta testers, otherwise more widely.

To make your screen sets available with a product, you can incorporate several screen sets into a screen filter program like the one in Appendix C. Screen filters imply development decisions: Is Adobe Accurate Screens the default or does it require special selection? How can users enable, disable, and bypass the filter? While these decisions don't directly affect the screen set, they affect its use.

Screen sets created for Adobe Accurate Screens software can be used directly by advanced users who choose to circumvent the screen filter. With application programs such as Adobe Photoshop, users can enter screen sets directly into dialog boxes. Screen sets can also be distributed in the form of Adobe Photoshop screen files, which the user selects from the appropriate dialog box. The screen set is then automatically loaded into the dialog box, avoiding transcription errors. Of course, screen sets can be incorporated into PostScript Printer Description (PPD) files for use with Adobe Illustrator™ and other illustration and page-layout programs.

You can also deliver screen sets as precalculated threshold arrays for downloading directly to the screen cache. This requires substantial technical expertise. Operation of the screen cache is a primary consideration with downloadable screen sets in certain RIPs with Adobe Accurate Screens software, because on these devices only a limited number of threshold arrays can be cached. To make sure downloaded threshold arrays are continuously available to users, they are locked—which prevents the RIP from deleting them from the screen cache to make room for newly calculated threshold arrays. This can make the output device operate slowly, because it must continually recalculate user-requested screens. Alert users to this issue, so they can decide how many of your precalculated threshold arrays to download, leaving screen cache space available if needed.

Ongoing development

Not long after your screen sets have been released, you will probably hear of "a problem with your screening." After investigating you may find that a press run failed due to a routine production error but your screen set is taking the blame. Expect this to happen. Since your screen set is the new kid on the block, it offers a convenient target whenever something goes wrong.

In some cases, however, your screen set may be the culprit. If so, do you plan to fix it, or will you let the marketplace decide what to do?

The rest of this chapter suggests a long-term development mechanism you can use to progressively improve your screening. Such a mechanism allows you to defend your screening from unwarranted claims of failure. It also allows you to provide high-quality field-tested information to your clients or customers.

Given the cost of producing and printing images, and the unacceptably high cost of failures, the printing trade prefers tried-and-true production methods. Trade shops that stand by their work often pay the bill when their work shows flaws. Where necessary, and as a normal cost of doing business, they remake jobs on a while-it-waits basis—paying for the costs incurred while the press is stopped, the image rescreened, flats restripped, plates reburned, and the press brought up to color again. In such circumstances they need to know *exactly* what to expect from your screen sets. They gain this tried-and-true information from experience: theirs or yours. If you want your screen sets widely used soon after their release, you need some level of ongoing development and organized field testing that gives users confidence in your screen sets.

For ongoing development you need to collect information about screen set performance in the field. It's best to beta test before general release. At least you need an organized system for gathering information.

When your screen sets perform well, there's no need to gather specific information (although samples might be in order). Where failure is suspected, the best single piece of information you can get is an *untrimmed* press sheet showing the problem and the quality control targets. If possible, get the negatives and plates. In a utopian situation you might get a transmittal form listing the press, inks, paper, and as much other information about the press run as possible—and an interview with the press operator soon after the job. This is a lot to ask, and you are unlikely to get it without an organized program involving sites that have agreed to provide such information in the event of suspected failures.

Given the material from the failed job and your filed negatives and press sheets from your screen set tests, you should be able to figure out what caused the failure. If the same problem shows up repeatedly, a statistical model may clarify the problem. (The more examples of a problem you obtain, the better off you are—from a statistical and research standpoint, at least).

Here are some possible problems:

- A tendency to develop patterns in the halftoned image can relate to any screen parameter. These may appear like moiré at first glance, but be related to dot structure, inking and other factors not directly related to screen superimposition.
- Tone reproduction problems are usually related to dot shape. You may need to rework the spot function or reconsider your dot shape approach.
- Artifacts you thought would remain invisible may emerge under specific conditions in the field. Few people are likely to care about this unless the artifacts are apparent to the unaided eye, but if artifacts are obvious you will have to issue an application bulletin or replace the screen set (or both).

If problems occur, you may be able to issue a bulletin or make a quick fix. More often you have to go back to the beginning, examine your quality criteria, and repeat the testing process before distributing a replacement screen set.

The long run

Over time you will build an impressive set of data related to your screen sets. You will learn what works best, and what to avoid. This process takes time, during which new output devices will be introduced. Each new device requires screen set testing, and your base of knowledge will make the process progressively more efficient.

APPENDICES

These Appendices contain three PostScript language
programs that have been used in the development of
screen sets: a search program for first-stage screen set
identification, a test page program for initial film testing,
and a prototype screen filter program. PostScript
language programmers can review these source listings
for ideas to incorporate into their own code. The three
programs are offered *as is*, as examples or as starter-kits,
with no guarantees that they will perform to your
expectations.

   If you elect to transcribe the programs, be prepared
to debug. Transcription errors cause PostScript language
errors. The most common error you will encounter is
undefined and the bad transcription will be listed as
OffendingCommand. The LaserTalk application is
well-suited for PostScript language programming and
debugging.

The three programs in these Appendices, with related
programs and refinements as developed, are available on
disk as the *Adobe Accurate Screens Screen Set Test Kit*.
The kit is available from *Desktop To Press*, Washington
DC, 800-551-5921. The kit, intended for commercial
screen set development, sells for $149.00, plus tax as
appropriate. A review kit with test page programs only is
available for $25.00, plus tax as appropriate. The cost in
either case does not include technical support.

APPENDIX A

Screen Set Search Program

The following program is designed to run on PostScript Level 1 RIPs that support the Level 1 Adobe Accurate Screens operators discussed in Chapter Eight. Instructions are included in comments in the program's header.

```
%!PS
%%Title: searchForAccurateScreenSets
%
% Copyright (c) 1991 and 1992 Adobe Systems Incorporated
% All rights reserved.
%
% NOTICE: This code is copyrighted by Adobe Systems Incorporated,
% and may not be reproduced for sale except by permission of Adobe
% Systems Incorporated. Adobe Systems Incorporated grants permission
% to use this code for the development of screen sets for use with Adobe
% Accurate Screens software, as long as the copyright notice remains intact.
%
% This program is designed to download to PostScript Level 1
% devices that support the Level 1 Accurate Screens operators.
% The program will not run successfully on other devices.
%
% This is a screen set search program based on traditional process-color
% screen assignments. You insert your screen set search criteria
% below, according to these instructions, and download the program to
% a PostScript Level 1 RIP that supports Adobe Accurate Screens
% software. The program delivers a report of screen sets that satisfy
% the criteria you have entered.
%
% This program's screen set report is delivered via the standard output
% channel of your RIP, to your workstation. To capture this output
% you should use Adobe's LaserTalk program or a functional
% equivalent. Capture the screen output and insert it into LaserTalk
% or a word processing file to generate hard copy output.
%
% To assign parameters in the USER DEFINABLE PARAMETERS area below:
%
% In the /angleA array, insert two, three, or four screen angles for inclusion
% in the screen set. If you are searching for screen sets to be used for
% standard process-color work with standard angles, leave the three values in
```

```
% the array as is.
%
% In the /freqA array, insert the beginning and ending points of the search
% range. This is the beginning LPI and ending LPI of the screen sets that will
% be reported.
%
% For the /AtLeast parameter, enter the desired Quality Index. In general a
% Quality Index of 100 or above indicates a screen set that merits
% investigation. Quality Index ratings of 400 to 600 have produced the best
% results to date. Very high Quality Index ratings indicate good, but not
% necessarily the best, screen sets.
%
% Leave the /frequencyStep parameter at 0.01 for thorough screen set searching.
% Coarser numbers may miss some screen sets. Finer numbers offer no
% advantage. All screen sets are found with the parameter at 0.01.
%
% The /maxlpi parameter protects you from inadvertently searching very small
% halftone cells. This parameter is the square root of the number of pixels in
% the cell. Set this parameter according to your smallest desired halftone
% cell.
%
% A screen space of 7, for the setscreenspace operator, is the default for most
% PostScript Level 1 RIPs. Increasing this value gives you more possible screen
% sets, but initial supercell calculations in the RIP will be longer whenever
% such screen sets are calculated via setscreen instead of being retrieved from
% the screen cache.
%
% Insert the desired search resolution. This need not be a resolution supported
% by the output device you are using for the search. The program will accept any
% typical resolution.
%
% The program can take a long time to execute, up to several hours in
% cases where the frequency range is wide. Thousands or tens of thousands
% of frequencies may need to be evaluated, which takes time. Try running the
% program overnight or specifying narrower frequency search ranges in /freqA.
%
% If using LaserTalk, increase its memory allocation to 1500K of RAM to allow
% long screen set reports to be received in the application's "PostScript
% Output" window. This is important when parameters are set in a manner that is
% likely to generate such reports, i.e. wide search ranges, low acceptable
% Quality Indexes, very fine frequency steps, etc.
%
% The program is written to emulate traditional screening. It assumes that
% deviations from requested screen parameters are "errors." This does not mean
% that screens are defective, only that they do not satisfy the particular
% screen combination theory used to write this particular search program.
%
%=============================================================
statusdict begin userdict begin
%=============================================================
%============ BEGIN USER DEFINABLE PARAMETERS =============
/angleA [15 45 75] def          % Angles to be searched (two, three or four)
/freqA [150 270] def            % Frequency range to be searched
/AtLeast 100 def                % Minimum acceptable Quality Index
/FrequencyStep 0.01 def         % Search interval in LPI
```

```
/maxlpi {resolution 8 div} def        % Minimum halftone cell side
7 setscreenspace                      % Screen space (from 7 to 16)
2400                                   % Resolution (not limited to search device)
%============ END USER DEFINABLE PARAMETERS ===============
% ==========================================================
{setresolution} stopped {statusdict /resolution 3 -1 roll put} if
% ==========================================================
%
% Internal procedures
%
/blankstring ( ) def
/str 10 string def
/fieldsize 5 def
/printflt                                       % num --    % Print as real/float
  {
  dup dup round eq
    {
    cvi
    } if
  dup cvi str cvs length fieldsize exch sub  % # leading blanks
  /leadin exch def
  blankstring 0 leadin getinterval print       % Print leading blanks
  str cvs dup print                            % Print the value
  length leadin add fieldsize 2 mul exch sub   % # trailing blanks
  blankstring 0 3 -1 roll getinterval print
  } bind def
/printint                                       % num -- % Print as integer
  {
  cvi
  dup str cvs length fieldsize exch sub         % # leading blanks
  /leadin exch def
  blankstring 0 leadin getinterval print        % Print leading blanks
  str cvs print                                 % Print the value
  } bind def
/tellme                                         % /name -- % Print name and its value
  {
  [ exch dup load exec ] ==
  } bind def
% ==========================================================
%
% More set-up
%
/numA angleA length def                % Number of angles in a set
/actFreqA numA array def               % Actual frequencies found in each try
/actAngleA numA array def              % Matching actual angles
%
pageparams setpageparams
true setaccuratescreens                % Can't forget this
%
% Report on all current and significant variables
%
(Searching for Accurate Screens screen sets\n) =
%
(Current RIP and program settings\n ) =
(Evaluated angles (angleA): ) print angleA ==
```

```
(Examined frequency ranges (freqA): ) print freqA ==
(Lowest acceptable QualityIndex (AtLeast): ) print AtLeast =
(Step size in search (FrequencyStep): ) print FrequencyStep =
(Device resolution: ) print resolution =
(Used screenspace: ) print screenspace =
(Amount of RAM memory: ) print ramsize =
(Status of accuratescreens: ) print accuratescreens =
(Software revision: ) print revision =
(Highest checked frequency: ) print maxlpi =
%
(\nGood frequencies [lpi] and resulting QualityIndexes [inches]:) =
%
% ============================================================
%
% Actually search for screen sets
%
0 2 freqA length 1 sub          % Try frequencies in every interval
  {
  %
  % Get the low and high frequency
  %
  /indx exch def
  /lo freqA indx get def
  /hi freqA indx 1 add get def
  lo hi gt
    {
    /hi lo /lo hi def def
    } if                        % Make sure low < hi
  hi maxlpi gt
    {
    /hi maxlpi def
    } if                              % Limit hi to maxlpi
  /lo lo FrequencyStep div round FrequencyStep mul def% Round-off errors
  /hi hi FrequencyStep div round FrequencyStep mul def% Round-off errors
  (\nTested interval: ) print [lo hi ] ==
  (Frequency Aggregate --- Actual frequency and angle values for each requested
angle --->) =
  ( to use QualityIndex ) print
  0 1 numA 1 sub
    {
    (| ) print
    angleA exch get printflt ( ) print
    } for
  (|) =
  %
  % Try all frequencies in this interval
  %
  lo FrequencyStep hi
    {
    %
    % Take out round-off errors
    %
    /f exch FrequencyStep div round FrequencyStep mul def
    %
    % Check 1 / aggregate QualityIndex < 1 / AtLeast
```

```
%
/maxerr 1 AtLeast 1e-10 add div def              % Max allowed error
/toterr 0 def                                    % Initialize aggregate error
0 1 numA 1 sub
   {
   /indx1 exch def
   %
   % Get resulting frequency and angle. Ignore QualityIndex
   %
   f angleA indx1 get checkscreen               % Frequency angle length
   pop actAngleA indx1 3 -1 roll put actFreqA indx1 3 -1 roll put
   %
   % Compare this to the previously calculated screens for this frequency
   %
   0 1 indx1 1 sub
      {
      /indx2 exch def
      %
      % CALCULATE THE ERROR
      %
      % Compute delta frequency and angle between two angles
      %
      /deltaf actFreqA indx1 get actFreqA indx2 get sub abs def
      %
      %   Check the angle errors
      %
      /deltaa actAngleA indx1 get angleA indx1 get sub
      actAngleA indx2 get angleA indx2 get sub sub abs def
      %
      % Total error is sqrt( deltaf^2 + (f*sin(deltaa))^2 )
      %
      /errorff deltaf dup mul f deltaa sin mul dup mul add sqrt def
      %
      % Error is 1 / QualityIndex
      % Save the largest error
      %
      errorff toterr gt
         {
         /toterr errorff def
         } if
      %
      % Exit to next frequency if error is too large
      %
      toterr maxerr gt
         {
         exit
         } if
      } for           % indx2
   %
   % Exit to next frequency if error is too large
   %
   toterr maxerr gt
      {
      exit
      } if
```

```
    } for        % indx1
  %
  % Evaluate and print out the results
  %
  toterr maxerr lt
    {
    f printflt ( ) print
    1 toterr 1e-10 add div        % Calculate the aggregate QualityIndex
    cvi printint ( ) print
    0 1 numA 1 sub
      {
      /indx exch def
      actFreqA indx get printflt
      actAngleA indx get printflt
      } for
    (\n) print
    } if
  } for           % f over lo..hi
} for             % lo..hi from freqA
% ============================================================
end end
```

Screen Set Film Test Program

This program provides a convenient way to generate the screen set test films discussed in Chapter Ten. In addition to the screen angle and screen frequencies, you can adjust screen space, page size, tint percentage, and dot shape.

```
%!PS
%
% Copyright (c) 1991 and 1992 Adobe Systems Incorporated
% All rights reserved.
%
% NOTICE: This code is copyrighted by Adobe Systems Incorporated,
% and may not be reproduced for sale except by permission of Adobe
% Systems Incorporated. Adobe Systems Incorporated grants permission
% to use this code for the development of screen sets for use with Adobe
% Accurate Screens software, as long as the copyright notice remains intact.
%
% By Peter Fink 1991/1992
%
% Use this PostScript program to generate sets of test pages for initial
% moiré testing of screen sets. This code generates test pages with large
% flat tints of 35% gray. Registration marks and automatic labeling are
% included. See "PostScript Screening: Adobe Accurate Screens" (Adobe Press,
% 1992) for details of how to use the output in screen set testing.
%
% This program does not require an Accurate Screens device. Pages contain a
% label to tell you whether Accurate Screens software was enabled when the
% file was run. If Accurate Screens software is enabled, the actual screen
% values are printed on the pages to the limit of decimal reporting accuracy in
% the RIP. If Accurate Screens software is not enabled, the requested screen
% values are printed on the pages.
%
% Insert screen frequency and screen angle parameters where indicated in the
% User Definable Parameters section below. You can also adjust the screen
% space, page size, tint percentage, and dot shape, and can add your own spot
% functions.
%
% In certain early drum units the page orientation may be wrong. If this occurs,
% change the /newLandscape boolean from false to true. This swaps the width and
% height page parameters.
```

```
%
%%%%%%%% BEGIN USER DEFINABLE PARAMETERS %%%%%%%%
%
/LPI1
  {
  133.1       % Set me
  } def
/Angle1
  {
  15          % Set me
  } def
%%%%%%%%%%%%%%%%%%%%%%
/LPI2
  {
  133.1       % Set me
  } def
/Angle2
  {
  45          % Set me
  } def
%%%%%%%%%%%%%%%%%%%%%%
/LPI3
  {
  133.1       % Set me
  } def
%
/Angle3
  {
  75          % Set me
  } def
%%%%%%%%%%%%%%%%%%%%%%
%
% Make zero degree screen about 108% of other LPI
%
/LPI4
  {
  143.5       % Set me
  } def
/Angle4
  {
  0           % Set me
  } def
%%%%%%%%%%%%%%%%%%%%%%
/screenSpace
  {
  7           % Set me
  } def
%%%%%%%%%%%%%%%%%%%%%%
/Dot
  {
  roundDot    % Set me
  } def
%%%%%%%%%%%%%%%%%%%%%%
/GrayValue    % Tint value, as setgray argument
  {
```

```
  .65          % Set me
  } def
%%%%%%%%%%%%%%%%%%%%
/PageWidth    % x dimension, outside edges of page
  {
  11 inch     % Set me
  } def
/PageHeight   % y dimension, outside edges of page
  {
  17 inch     % Set me
  } def
/newLandscape % Change to true if page orientation wrong, otherwise false
  {
  false       % Set me
  } def
%%%%%%%%%%%%%%%%%%%%
%
% SPOT FUNCTIONS
%
/roundDot
  {
    {
    dup mul exch dup mul add 1 exch sub
    } bind
  } def
%
/squareDot                           % Also called Euclidean dot
  {
    {
    abs exch abs 2 copy add 1 gt
      {
      1 sub dup mul exch 1 sub dup mul add 1
      sub
      }
      {
      dup mul exch dup mul add 1 exch sub
      } ifelse
    } bind
  } def
%
/diamondDot
  {
    {
    abs exch abs 2 copy add .75 le       % Round spot to diamond
      {
      dup mul exch dup mul add 1 exch sub
      }
      {
      2 copy add 1.23 le                 % Diamonds to round spots
        {
        .76 mul add 1 exch sub           % Width of diamonds
        }
        {
        1 sub dup mul exch 1 sub dup mul add 1 sub
        }
```

```
        ifelse
        } ifelse
      } bind
    } def
%
%%%%%%%%% END USER-DEFINABLE PARAMETERS %%%%%%%%%
%
% Other procedures
%
/bdf {bind def} def
%
/DoPrecise                    % Align with device pixels
  {
  transform round exch round exch itransform
  /yPrecise exch def /xPrecise exch def
  } bdf
%
/inch
  {
  72 mul
  } bdf
%
/LLx                    % For translating whole page only
  {
  0
  } def
%
/LLy                    % For translating whole page only
  {
  0
  } def
%
/Xpos                   % Initial value of Xpos; changes during program
  {
  .5 inch
  } bdf
%
/Ypos                   % Initial value of Ypos; changes during program
  {
  .5 inch
  } bdf
%
/xBoxSide               % Square box
  {
  PageWidth 1 inch sub
  } bdf
%
/yBoxSide               % Square box
  {
  PageHeight 1 inch sub
  } bdf
%
/doBox
  {dup 0 exch rlineto exch 0 rlineto neg 0 exch rlineto closepath fill} bdf
%
```

150

```
/DoTintBox1                              % Translated; uses some above def's
  {
  gsave
  Xpos Ypos moveto
  xBoxSide yBoxSide doBox
  0 setgray
  Xpos .1 inch add Ypos .1 inch add moveto
  statusdict /accuratescreens known
      {
      statusdict begin accuratescreens
        {
        (Accurate Screens: ON ) show
        currentscreen pop exch
        8 string cvs show ( LPI, ) show
        8 string cvs show ( Degrees) show
        }
        {
        (Accurate Screens: OFF ) show
        LPI1 8 string cvs show ( Requested LPI, ) show
        Angle1 8 string cvs show ( Requested Degrees) show
        }
      ifelse
      end                                % statusdict
      }
      {
      (Accurate Screens Unavailable ) show
      LPI1 8 string cvs show ( Requested LPI, ) show
      Angle1 8 string cvs show ( Requested Degrees) show
      }
  ifelse
  grestore
  } bdf
%
/DoTintBox2                              % Translated; uses some above def's
  {
  gsave
  Xpos Ypos moveto
  xBoxSide yBoxSide doBox
  0 setgray
  Xpos .1 inch add Ypos .1 inch add moveto
  statusdict /accuratescreens known
      {
      statusdict begin accuratescreens
        {
        (Accurate Screens: ON ) show
        currentscreen pop exch
        8 string cvs show ( LPI, ) show
        8 string cvs show ( Degrees) show
        }
        {
        (Accurate Screens: OFF ) show
        LPI2 8 string cvs show ( Requested LPI, ) show
        Angle2 8 string cvs show ( Requested Degrees) show
        }
      ifelse
```

```
      end                              % statusdict
      }
      {
      (Accurate Screens Unavailable ) show
      LPI2 8 string cvs show ( Requested LPI, ) show
      Angle2 8 string cvs show ( Requested Degrees) show
      }
  ifelse
  grestore
  } bdf
%
/DoTintBox3                           % Translated; uses some above def's
  {
  gsave
  Xpos Ypos moveto
  xBoxSide yBoxSide doBox
  0 setgray
  Xpos .1 inch add Ypos .1 inch add moveto
  statusdict /accuratescreens known
     {
     statusdict begin accuratescreens
       {
       (Accurate Screens: ON ) show
       currentscreen pop exch
       8 string cvs show ( LPI, ) show
       8 string cvs show ( Degrees) show
       }
       {
       (Accurate Screens: OFF ) show
       LPI3 8 string cvs show ( Requested LPI, ) show
       Angle3 8 string cvs show ( Requested Degrees) show
       }
     ifelse
     end                              % statusdict
     }
     {
     (Accurate Screens Unavailable ) show
     LPI3 8 string cvs show ( Requested LPI, ) show
     Angle3 8 string cvs show ( Requested Degrees) show
     }
  ifelse
  grestore
  } bdf
%
/DoTintBox4                           % Translated; uses some above def's
  {
  gsave
  Xpos Ypos moveto
  xBoxSide yBoxSide doBox
  0 setgray
  Xpos .1 inch add Ypos .1 inch add moveto
  statusdict /accuratescreens known
     {
     statusdict begin accuratescreens
       {
```

```
     (Accurate Screens: ON ) show
     currentscreen pop exch
     8 string cvs show ( LPI, ) show
     8 string cvs show ( Degrees) show
     }
     {
     (Accurate Screens: OFF ) show
     LPI4 8 string cvs show ( Requested LPI, ) show
     Angle4 8 string cvs show ( Requested Degrees) show
     }
   ifelse
   end                             % statusdict
   }
   {
   (Accurate Screens Unavailable ) show
   LPI4 8 string cvs show ( Requested LPI, ) show
   Angle4 8 string cvs show ( Requested Degrees) show
   }
 ifelse
 grestore
 } bdf
%
/Circle
 {
 0 360 arc stroke
 } bdf
%
/RegMark                          % Used within RegistrationMarks procedure
 {
 translate
 newpath
 0 setgray
 .005 inch setlinewidth
 0 1 3
   {
   /counter exch def 0 0 .12 inch counter .02 inch mul sub Circle
   } for
 newpath
 0 0 moveto
 -.25 inch 0 rmoveto .5 inch 0 rlineto stroke
 0 0 moveto
 0 -.25 inch rmoveto 0 .5 inch rlineto stroke
 } bdf
%
/RegistrationMarks
 {
 %
 % Lower Left Registration Mark
 %
 gsave .4 inch .4 inch RegMark grestore
 %
 % Upper Left Registration Mark
 %
 gsave .4 inch PageHeight .4 inch sub RegMark grestore
 %
```

```
  % Lower Right Registration Mark
  %
  gsave PageWidth .4 inch sub .4 inch RegMark grestore
  %
  % Upper Right Registration Mark
  %
  gsave PageWidth .4 inch sub PageHeight .4 inch sub RegMark grestore
  } bdf
%
% End of procedures
%
% Begin pages
%
statusdict /accuratescreens known
  {statusdict begin
  true setaccuratescreens screenSpace setscreenspace
  PageWidth PageHeight
  newLandscape                      % Correction for early drum pageparams
    {
    exch
    }
  if
  0 0
  setpageparams
  end            % statusdict
  }
if
%
/Helvetica findfont 10 scalefont setfont
GrayValue setgray
%%%%%%%%%%%%%%%%%%%%%%%%%%%%%%%% FILMSET
%
%%%%%%%%%%%%%%%%%%%%%%%%%%%%%%%% PAGE ONE
LPI1 Angle1 Dot setscreen
LLx LLy translate
GrayValue setgray
DoTintBox1
RegistrationMarks
showpage
%%%%%%%%%%%%%%%%%%%%%%%%%%%%%%%% PAGE TWO
LPI2 Angle2 Dot setscreen
LLx LLy translate
GrayValue setgray
DoTintBox2
RegistrationMarks
showpage
%%%%%%%%%%%%%%%%%%%%%%%%%%%%%%%% PAGE THREE
LPI3 Angle3 Dot setscreen
LLx LLy translate
GrayValue setgray
DoTintBox3
RegistrationMarks
showpage
%%%%%%%%%%%%%%%%%%%% PAGE FOUR (higher LPI, zero degrees)
LPI4 Angle4 Dot setscreen
```

```
LLx LLy translate
GrayValue setgray
DoTintBox4
RegistrationMarks
showpage
%%%%%%%%%%%%%%%%%%%%%%%%%%%%%% END PAGES
```

Screen Filter Program

This screen filter program is designed for use by equipment vendors and expert PostScript language programmers. To use it effectively you should have detailed information regarding your device's PostScript language implementation. Such information may not be available to the general public. Contact your vendor for details.

Even if you do not use this code in an implementation, if you are a PostScript language programmer you can learn much about screen filter operation by studying this program carefully.

```
%!PS
%%Title: screenfilter.ps
%
% Copyright (c) 1991 and 1992 Adobe Systems Incorporated
% All rights reserved.
%
% NOTICE: This code is copyrighted by Adobe Systems Incorporated,
% and may not be reproduced for sale except by permission of Adobe
% Systems Incorporated. Adobe Systems Incorporated grants permission
% to use this code for the development of screen sets for use with Adobe
% Accurate Screens software, as long as the copyright notice remains intact.
%
%% Download file
%
%serverdict begin 0 exitserver        % for Sys/, FC/, and DB/ files
%
/download                             % (filename) --
  {
  (w) file/fut exch def               % Output file
  (%stdin) (r) file/fin exch def      % Input file
  /str512 512 string def
    {
    fin str512 readstring not /done exch def
    fut exch writestring
    done
      {
      exit
      } if
    } loop
```

```
  fut closefile
  fin closefile
  } bind def
%
%here: (%diskn%filename) download
%
(Adobe/screenfilter) download
% =============================================================
%
% This file implements a screen filter for PostScript Level 1 Emerald
% imagesetters that support Accurate Screens software.
%
% The filter handles calls to setscreen and setcolorscreen. If the frequency
% and angle are integers, Accurate Screens and the filter are turned on;
% then the filter modifies the screen frequency. If screen frequency is
% expressed to any decimal, the user's screen request is honored.
% The angle is never converted. The filter must be fed proper
% replacement values in screentable0 below.
%
% Additional operators in userdict:
%
%     screenfilter   returns boolean true if filter is on
%     boolean setscreenfilter   sets screenfilter
%
% Include this file name in the Sys/Bootlist file
%
% =============================================================
%
% Visible entries in userdict
%
userdict begin
%
/screenfilter                    % -- boolean % true = filter is on
  {
  screenfilterdict begin
  screenfilterflag
  end
  } bind def
%
/setscreenfilter                 % boolean or int -- % true or 2 turns filter on
  {
  dup type /integertype eq       % Accept 2 for compatibility reasons
    {
    2 eq
    } if
  dup type /booleantype eq
    {
    screenfilterdict /setfilterflag 3 -1 roll put
    }
    {
    pop                          % Ignore or raise a typecheck
    } ifelse
  } bind def
%
/setscreen                       % frequency angle procedure --
```

```
{
2 index dup cvi eq                          % f is int
screenfilter and                            % Filter is on
statusdict /accuratescreens get exec and    % Accurate Screens is on
   {
   screenfilterdict begin
   filterScreen
   end
   } if
systemdict /setscreen get exec
} bind def
%
/setcolorscreen                    % 4 sets of frequency angle procedure -
-
   {
   4
      {
      2 index dup cvi eq                       % f is int
      screenfilter and                         % Filter is on
      statusdict /accuratescreens get exec and % Accurate Screens is on
         {
         screenfilterdict begin
         filterScreen
         end
         } if
      12 3 roll                                % Roll up the next screen set
      } repeat
   systemdict /setcolorscreen get exec
   } bind def
%
/screenfilterdict 20 dict def
%
end                    % userdict
% ==========================================================
%
% Private entries in screenfilterdict
%
screenfilterdict begin
%
/filterScreen          % frequency angle procedure -- frequency angle procedure
   {
   /proc exch def /angle exch def /freq exch def
   /res statusdict begin resolution end def
   /spc statusdict begin screenspace end def
   freq freq screenfilterwidth mul 2 copy add /fh exch def sub /fl exch def
   %
   % Search for the right screentable based on the angle
   %
   screentables                            % forall
      {
      /subtab exch def
      /tabletouse subtab 0 get def
      %
      % Search for the matching angle
      %
```

```
      false
      subtab 1 get
         {
         angle cvi 900 add 90 mod eq
            {
            pop true exit
            } if
         } forall
   %
   % Did we find a good screen table?
   %
      {
      %
      % Search this screentable for matching resolution and screenspace
      %
      /foundAtSpace 0 def                    % no freq found yet
      tabletouse load                        % forall
         {
         /subtab exch def
         spc subtab 1 get ge foundAtSpace subtab 1 get lt and
                        %
                        % foundAtSpace < needed space < spc
                        %
         res subtab 0 get eq and
            {
            %
            % This subtable is applicable; search it for good frequencies
            %
            subtab 2 get                   % forall
               {
               /fx exch def
               fx fl ge fx fh le and               % fl <= fx <= fh ==> MATCH
                  {
                  %
                  % Use fx as new freq
                  %
                  /freq fx def /foundAtSpace subtab 1 get def exit
                  } if
               } forall                    % Frequency array
            } if                           % subtab is applicable
         } forall                          % tabletouse
      %
      % Return updated parameters
      %
      } if                                 % Found a screentable
   } forall                                % Search for a screentable
   freq angle /proc load
   } bind def
% ============================================================================
%
% The following entries are to be defined by the adapter of this filter:
%
/screenfilterflag true def                          % default value true or false
%
/screenfilterwidth 0.03 def                        % + or - 3 percent
```

```
%
% Multiple screen tables can be used/selected by the incoming angle
%
/screentables
[ % table [ screen angles covered by this table ]
[ /screentable0 [ 0 15 45 75 ]]
] def
%
% The following table and subtables must be entered with accurate numbers.
% Enter one line for each combination of resolution and screenspace.
%   Example: [ 2400 17 [ 98.345 134.782 199.002 ]]
%   Example: [ 2400 7 [ 99.300 112.141 175.012 ]]
%
% THE FOLLOWING ARE NOT PROVEN SCREEN SETS.
% THEY ARE INCLUDED FOR ILLUSTRATION PURPOSES ONLY.
%
/screentable0                        % screen table for 0,15, 45, 75 degrees
[ % resolution, screenspace, [ good frequencies for 0,15, 45, 75 angle set ]
[ 600 7 [ ]]
[ 1000 7 [ ]]
[ 1016 7 [ ]]
[ 1200 7 [ ]]
[ 1270 7 [ ]]
[ 1625 7 [ ]]
[ 2048 7 [ ]]
[ 2400 7 [ 81.2 90.91 98.25 106.07 121.21 136.37 145.46 155.29 166.67
          181.82 188.57 195.35]]
[ 2400 10 [83.34 99.25 110.92 132.81 152.39 175.28 198.35 ]]
[ 2400 16 [80.62 89.65 92.9 100.32 107.46 115.86 120.71 125.43
          134.482 147.95 153.695 161.08 175.28 185.81 192.45 201.2 208.22]]
[ 2540 7 [ ]]
[ 3072 7 [ ]]
[ 3251 7 [ ]]
] def
%
end                                  % screenfilterdict
%
%============================================================
%
% Some test cases:
%
% statusdict begin true setaccuratescreens 10 setscreenspace end letter
%
% 85 45 {pop} setscreen 100 45 {pop} setscreen
% 120 45 {pop} setscreen 133 45 {pop} setscreen
% 150 45 {pop} setscreen 175 45 {pop} setscreen 200 45 {pop} setscreen
%
```

Bibliography

The reference materials are organized by topic. Telephone numbers are included for small publishers who may be difficult to reach by other means.

Color Theory and Production

Bann, David, and John Gargan. *How to Check and Correct Color Proofs.* Cincinnati: North Light Books, 1990. Process color production with emphasis on fine color adjustments in CMYK.

Bruno, Michael H. *Principles of Color Proofing.* Salem, NH: GAMA Communications, 1986. 603-898-2822. Comprehensive, moderately technical discussion of conventional proofing methods.

Hunt, R.W.G. *The Reproduction of Colour in Photography, Printing & Television.* 4th. ed. Tolworth, England: Fountain Press, 1987. Thorough technical treatment of color, tone, and vision.

Hunter, Richard S. *The Measurement of Appearance.* John Wiley & Sons, 1987. Mathematical textbook, color and surface effects.

Molla, R. K. *Electronic Color Separation.* Montgomery, WV: R. K. Printing & Publishing Company, 1988. Lightly technical discussion of halftoning, digital halftoning, color, and scanning.

Southworth, Miles, and Thad McIlroy and Donna Southworth. *The Color Resource Complete Color Glossary.* Livonia, NY: The Color Resource, 1992. 800-724-9476. Thorough overview of terminology. Catalog of many related titles available.

Wyszecki, Günter. *Color Science.* John Wiley & Sons, 1982. Highly mathematical textbook.

General

Hamilton, Jim. *Linotype-Hell Technical Information.* 425 Oser Avenue, Hauppauge, NY 11788. Extensive series of lightly technical articles on PostScript language imagesetting and related topics.

Desktop To Press. Washington, DC: Peter Fink Communications, Inc. 800-551-5921. Periodical. Articles relating to PostScript language imagesetting, halftones, and prepress production. Catalog of titles available.

What's New(s) in Graphic Communications. 5129 Wedge Court East, Bradenton, FL 34203: Michael H. Bruno, 813-756-6673. Bimonthly periodical. Commentary and abstracts of technical conferences worldwide.

Halftone and Moiré

All of the sources in this section are highly technical.

Bryngdahl, O. "Moiré Formation and Interpretation" *J. Opt. Soc. America*, 64, no. 10 (1974): 1287-1294. Mathematical theory of moiré formation and forecasting method.

Delabastita, Paul. "Screening Techniques and Moiré in Four Color Printing." To be published as part of the April 1992 TAGA conference proceedings by the Technical Association for the Graphic Arts (TAGA), October 1992. Basis for AGFA Balanced Screening. See address in the following section: "Sources for Quality-Control Devices, Test Suites, and Printing Technologies."

Eschbach, Roger. "Generation of Moiré by Nonlinear Transfer Characteristics." *J. Opt. Soc. Am. A.* 5, no. 11 (November 1988). Highly mathematical discussion of nonlinear tone dependencies in formation of moiré.

Tollenaar, D. "Moiré Interference Phenomena in Halftone Printing." Amsterdam, The Netherlands: Research Institute T.N.O. for Printing and Allied Industries, 1945. Original publication in Dutch. English translation published with updated references by Research and Engineering Council of the USA, 1957. Landmark, highly mathematical analysis of moiré.

Ulichney, Robert. *Digital Halftoning.* Cambridge, MA: MIT Press, 1987. Highly mathematical book based on MIT Ph.D. thesis. Ninety references include most significant books and articles in the field as of the date of publication.

Photographic Theory, Tone, and Production

Adams, Ansel. *Examples: The Making of 40 Photographs*. Boston: Little, Brown & Company (Bulfinch Press), 1983. Lightly technical discussions of tone in specific circumstances.

Adams, Ansel. *The New Ansel Adams Photography Series*. 3 Vols., *The Camera, The Negative, The Print*. Boston: Little, Brown & Company, 1981. Classic discussion of tone and tone management in conventional photography.

Eaton, George T. *Photographic Chemistry*, 4th. ed. Dobbs Ferry, NY: Morgan & Morgan, 1986. Moderately technical (chemistry) discussion.

Advanced Black-and-White Photography. Kodak Publication No. KW-19. Eastman Kodak Company, 1987. Sensitometry, tone, and practical tone management in conventional photography.

Kodak Professional Black-and-White Films. Kodak Publication No. F-5. Eastman Kodak Company, 1987. Sensitometry, tone, and practical tone management in conventional photography.

Quality Enlarging. Kodak Publication No. G-1. Eastman Kodak Company, 1985. Sensitometry, tone, and practical tone management in conventional photography.

Sanders, Norman. *Photographing for Publication*. R.R. Bowker Company, 1983. Very accessible, lightly technical treatment of photography and offset lithography.

PostScript Language Reference and Education

Holzgang, David. *PostScript Programmer's Reference Guide*. Scott, Foresman and Company, 1989. Overview of PostScript Level 1 language.

Reid, Glenn C. *PostScript Language Program Design*. Addison-Wesley, 1988. Technical discussion of PostScript language programming including half-tone-related code.

Roth, Stephen F., ed. *Real World PostScript*. Addison-Wesley, 1988. Lightly technical introduction to PostScript language programming and RT Screening.

Smith, Ross. *Learning PostScript: A Visual Approach*. Berkeley, CA: Peachpit Press, 1990. Lightly technical introduction to PostScript programming.

PostScript Language Reference Manual. 2nd ed. Addison-Wesley, 1990. Essential technical reference for PostScript language, both Level 1 and Level 2.

PostScript Printer Description File Format Specification, Version 4.0. Adobe Developer's Association, Mountain View, CA. 415-961-4111.

Printing Technology

Beach, Mark, and Steve Shapiro and Ken Russon. *Getting It Printed*. Portland, OR: Coast To Coast Books, 1986. Concise introduction to prepress production.

Blair, Roy, ed. *The Lithographer's Manual*. Pittsburgh: Graphic Arts Technical Foundation, 1988. Detailed summary of current printing practices.

Brehm, Peter V. *Introduction to Densitometry*. Alexandria, VA: Graphic Communications Association, 1990. Comprehensive, moderately technical discussion of densitometry.

Southworth, Miles, and Donna Southworth. *Quality and Productivity in the Graphic Arts*. Livonia, NY: The Color Resource, 1989. Thorough, moderately technical discussion of quality control considerations, techniques, and targets. Ample references and resource list.

Leach, R.H, et al. eds. *The Printing Ink Manual*, 4th. ed. London: Van Nostrand Reinhold (International), 1988. Highly technical. Chemistry and physics of printing and printing inks. Extensive references are mostly European.

Sources for Quality-Control Devices, Test Suites, and Printing Technology

The following sources offer a wide range of books, instructional materials, technical research reports, quality control test forms, and test suites. Catalogs are available.

Graphic Arts Technical Foundation (GATF). 4615 Forbes Avenue, Pittsburgh, PA 15213-3796. 412-621-6941.

Graphic Communications Association (GCA). 100 Daingerfield Road, Alexandria, VA 22314-2888. 703-519-8160, FAX 703-548-2867.

GCA/Adobe PostScript Data Device Test Suite. Available 4th quarter, 1992 from the GCA PostScript test suite, ideal for screen set development.

Accurate Screens Screen Set Test Kit. Desktop To Press, Washington, DC. 800-551-5921. Disk of PostScript language search tools, test pages, spot function test pages, and related code for first-stage screen set identification and testing.

Rochester Institute of Technology (RIT), Technical and Education Center of the Graphic Arts. P.O Box 9887, Rochester, NY 14623. 716-475-2737.

Technical Association of the Graphic Arts (TAGA). P.O Box 9887, Rochester, NY 14623. 716-272-0557, FAX 716-475-2250. Proceedings of annual conferences with technical papers.

Tools of the Trade. 3718 Seminary Road, Alexandria, VA 22304. 703-683-4186. Mail order retailer. Unusually wide selection of books on graphic arts, desktop publishing, and printing, from basic to highly technical.

System Brunner USA Inc. 12 Harbor Lane, Rye, NY 10580. 914-381-4842. Comprehensive system of quality-control targets.

Index

of screen sets,   120–121
test targets for,   128–129
Quantization,   77, 97–98
    and cell balancing,   78
    with clustered dot dithering,   24
    as error,   88
    and halftone cells,   79–84
    and rational tangents,   85–87
    and screen generation,   79–87

Range of tones,   6–8, 134
Raster devices,   16–17
Rational tangents,   85–88
Recorders,   28
Reference materials, bibliography for,   163–167
Reflected light,   5
Registration problems,   38, 122
Registration targets,   128
Relationships, tonal,   7–8
Resolution
    of dither patterns,   20
    of imagesetters,   29
    and pixel addressability,   18
    of raster devices,   18
Rhomboid dots,   67–68, 73–74
RIP (raster image processor),   28–29
Roll-feed transport mechanisms,   28
Roller problems,   35
ROM problems,   33
Rosette structures,   49–51
    color tone ramps for,   129
    consistency in,   54
    in screen sets,   111–113, 120, 122–124
    spot functions with,   74
    three-screen,   52–53
Rotated angle sets,   116
Round dots,   64–69, 71
RT Screening
    and halftone cells,   79–84
    vs. supercell screening,   95

Saturation of color,   5–6
Scan lines,   18
Screen caches,   29–30
Screen filters,   30, 114–115, 135, 157–161
Screen sets,   30, 97–98, 102
    black angle in,   114–115
    calibrating output chains for,   121–122
    criteria for,   120
    development process for,   107–108
    dot structures in,   125
    evaluating,   109–110
    film test program for,   147–155
    high frequencies in,   116–117

libraries of,   103
moiré patterns in,   111–113, 120, 122–124
for one-color screens,   126
ongoing development of,   136–137
releasing,   135–136
rosette structures for,   111–113, 120, 122–124
rotated angle sets for,   116
screen combination theories for,   111
screen filters for,   114, 135, 157–161
vs. screen technology,   109
searching for,   108, 121, 141–146
selecting,   119–126
shade-stepping in,   126
spot functions for,   113–114, 124–125
testing,   108–109, 127–135
traditional frequencies for,   115–116
yellow frequency in,   112–113
Screens
    assignments for,   57–60
    and 15-degree moiré pattern,   54–56
    frequency of, and quantization,   78
    generating,   79–87
    from grids,   51–52
    misalignment of, and moiré period,   53–54
    swapping,   58–60, 112–113
screenspace operator,   103–104, 106
Scumming,   39
Searching for screen sets,   108, 121, 141–146
Secondary moiré patterns,   43
Selecting screen sets,   119–126
setaccuratescreens operator,   103–104
sethalftone operator,   103, 105
setscreen operator,   71, 74, 103, 105, 114
setscreenspace operator,   104
Shade-stepping
    and banding,   33
    with clustered dot dithering,   24
    in press tests,   134–135
    and quantization effects,   77
    in screen sets,   126
Shadow behavior,   69
Shadow detail in press tests,   134
Shape of dots. See Dot shape
Simple round dots,   65, 70–71
Size
    of bitmaps,   29
    of color images,   120
    of dots (See Dot gain)
    of pixels,   18–19, 22
    of supercells,   95
Spatial quantization,   77–78
Spot functions
    bind operator with,   74–75